THE FATE
OF OTTO SCHOLZ

An Imperial Berliner in a British War Hospital

DR SIMON DANIELS

COPYRIGHT

Powerhouse Publications
Suite 124. 94 London Road
Headington, Oxford
OX3 9FN

www.powerhousepublishing.com

Otto Scholz

CONTENTS

INTRODUCTION

You would never expect one of the greatest untold dramas of the First World War right on your doorstep. Certainly, you would never think that there were any secrets lurking in the Royal Victoria Country Park, on the edge of Southampton Water in Southern England. You might have just moved here, and found it by accident, on a sunny day when people are strolling or relaxing with friends and family, none of them any the wiser of the history either. If you did not know better, the towering dome of the restored Chapel, right in the middle, seems to be a bit of a folly. Yet, a hundred years ago, the Chapel would have been the only thing you recognised. The awesome façade of The Royal Victoria Military Hospital stretched for a quarter of a mile along the shore-line, a gigantic building of red brick and stone, over which the dome of that Chapel towered broodingly. Ambulance trains arrived endlessly from hospital ships, full of wounded soldiers, blinded, maimed, dying, still caked in Flanders mud. They even had to build a town of wooden huts in the grounds as the Hospital overflowed.

In June 2014, the BBC broadcast a documentary programme about the experience of Netley Hospital in the First World War. It was distressing and compelling at the same time, bringing into public view the battles that were fought on the Home Front, with story lines that were rooted in the Hospital's own experience. The final story was, perhaps, the most riveting. Otto Scholz was a young man who had hopes and plans for an aristocratic life in Imperial Berlin, but fate had very different plans, as he crossed the Belgian border with his Regiment in August, 1914, only to be wounded and taken prisoner a month later. He then disappeared from view until he died at this vast military hospital at Netley, in December 1916. Just what had been the fate of this young man, who had the promise of such a glittering life?

That was the question which drove me to write this book. It started when I was first introduced to the park; wandering through the cemetery and its silent ranks of war graves, I encountered an unusual one with a regulation headstone, at the foot of a granite cross. I read the inscription, in German, in memory of Otto Paul Carl Scholz, a Lieutenant in the 3rd Prussian Regiment of Lancers, born in Berlin in 1890, who died as a prisoner of war at Netley in December 1916. It was intriguing because it was unique, giving just enough information to ask myself, what had happened to him, that led him to be here. It was the very question I asked the park manager; she replied: *"We don't know, but if you can find out anything, please let us know."*

It has taken thirty years to answer that. This is the story of that young man, those who fought with him, and those who tried to stop him, in the first month of the war. This gives us a vivid picture of how he got here; now we must ask questions about his fate. It is far from a dry biography or just another history book, but a detective story that must place the evidence in context. For this, we need to make sense of the First World War through the eyes and fears of a military hospital, and how it had to meet the demands of a war that kept pressing for ever-greater leaps in medical science, to save maimed bodies and shattered minds. However they met those demands, the secrets were buried deep; that is why it has taken thirty years.

Since I was featured in that BBC documentary in 2014, it has been broadcast a number of times and, every time, I have been approached by viewers – often strangers in the street - who want to know more about his fate. It is as if people have questions in their own mind, which have formed around suspicions about his treatment at Netley, for which they need answers. And that is where you come in. Mark Twain said that a successful book is not made by what is *in* it, but what is left *out* of it. This book sets out the evidence, analyses what we know and sets it in the context of the world in which the people were living at the time. It is for you, though, to consider your verdict, according to the evidence.

IMPERIAL GERMANY:
IF I CANNOT INSPIRE LOVE,
I WILL CAUSE FEAR[1]

It is an incredibly hard task to make sense of why the First World War took place at all. Europe had been flourishing in the years of peace following the Franco-Prussian War, while the *Pax Britannica* of Britain's Imperial Century was not just a physical reality but a state of mind. So, what went wrong? To make a start on answering this question, we need to picture the right opening scene. Perhaps, that is the scene of Queen Victoria's deathbed.

The Queen-Empress was eighty-six years old, and the New Year of 1901 barely a month, as she lay in her bed at Osborne House, on the Isle of Wight, convulsed by a series of strokes. She passed quite peacefully, on the 22nd January, quitting a reign of nearly 64 years, and leaving a legacy of 37 surviving great-grandchildren uniting a Continent. She had married them well, earning the sobriquet the Matriarch of Europe which forged the bonds that kept the Crowned Heads at peace. She died surrounded by her family – and, notably, the two figures who would squander her legacy – her son, who would succeed her as King Edward VII, and her grandson, Kaiser Wilhelm II. *The Economist* reflected on the genuine sorrow of her people at the death of the Queen-Empress and observed that the nation would never see such a golden era of Imperial Greatness again[2]. How prophetic that

---

[1] Spoken by The Monster in *Frankenstein; or, The Modern Prometheus*, by Mary Shelley

[2] See www.economist.com/news/21663911-what-we-wrote-her-passing-1901-death-queen-victoria

would become, although not, perhaps, in the way envisaged. The death of the Matriarch of Europe loosened those bonds between the Crowned Heads of Europe; without such a Sovereign to bind them, the era could only have closed, and, eventually, bring the same peoples to war.

In fairness, perhaps the causes of the war were born a generation before, while the Queen-Empress was presiding over the Nation's Glory – but the causes had very little to do with Great Britain. In 1870, amid the glorious high-water mark of French nineteenth century culture, a problem had presented itself when the vacant throne of Spain was offered to a branch of the ruling house of Prussia. France was growing nervous about the growth of Prussian power over the subordinate states in Germany's Confederation under Bismarck's expert pilotage; it hardly wanted to be surrounded by Hoenzollern crowned heads, and immediately lodged a strong protest. On Bismarck's advice, the offer of the throne was refused; but that was not enough for the French who appeared conceited, even antagonistic, in demanding further assurances.

In the summer of 1870, the King Wilhelm I was taking the waters at the spa town of Ems, where he met with the French ambassador, Count Vincent Benedetti, who demanded Wilhelm's guarantee that the candidacy of a Hohenzollern to the Spanish throne would never be renewed. The King politely refused to go that far, and the audience ended. Benedetti subsequently asked for a further interview, but Wilhelm instructed his personal Aide de Camp, in accordance with protocol, to inform Benedetti that he had no further communication to make to him.

A telegram reporting the interview was then sent to Bismarck in Berlin. The Chancellor sent an edited version of the despatch to the press next day in the usual way, which, however, omitted the diplomatic courtesies and Wilhelm's conciliatory response to the French persistence. Fatally, the French translation by the agency Havas incorrectly transposed the French equivalent of a non-commissioned officer for Aide de Camp, implying that the King had deliberately insulted the ambassador by not choosing a senior officer to carry the message to him. By sad coincidence, the newspapers carried the mistranslation on the 14th July, Bastille Day, France's national day. Amid the high-water mark of French prestige, Bismarck's despatch humiliated the French people, whose wounded pride demanded satisfaction and, on the 19th July, France declared war. One small voice of dissent came from the French ambassador in Washington: *You will not go to Germany, but be crushed in France. Believe me, for I know the Prussian.* Then he committed suicide.

In many ways, the Franco-Prussian War brought the German war machine to its maturity. It was a tribute to the philosophy of a long-dead Prussian soldier who, yet, was studied in the finest military academies in the world. Carl von Clausewitz had joined the Prussian Army in 1792, aged 12, and he died a general in 1831. In fact, almost in mimicry of a Christian saint, his greatest triumph was not achieved until after his death; his widow, it was, who published his collected works on military theory, *On War*, which is still studied today. Its philosophy stripped away the myths of 'civilized' warfare:

We are not interested in generals who win victories without bloodshed. The fact that slaughter is a horrifying spectacle must make us take war more seriously, but not provide an excuse for gradually blunting our swords in the name of humanity. Sooner or later someone will come along with a sharp sword and hack off our arms[3].

---

[3] Clausewitz, C, 1832, On War, unfinished but published posthumously by his widow; author's translation.

Clausewitz's words had really struck home to the Prussian Officer Corps, who took the declaration of war very seriously indeed, unlike their French counterparts who marched eastwards thinking it all a splendid adventure into glory; they had no understanding of the military professionalism that they would be up against. Within weeks the Prussian Army was besieging Paris after a brilliant campaign in which it had enjoyed full support from the armies of all the German states, bringing Unification and causing the rest of the world to rethink its views on the Balance of Power in Europe.

Following France's humiliation with the end of the war against Prussia in May 1871, the French had to pay war reparations of five billion francs, a massive sum which the Germans confidently thought would keep the French occupied in peace for generations. But more than that, France had to cede to Germany the treasured possessions of Alsace and Lorraine, sacred to the French heart, not just for their beauty but also for their wealth of coal and steel. The French murmured *Revanche* and bided their time.

Germany had financed its war effort for the Franco-Prussian War by issuing war loans and the reparations were promptly used to repay the loans as promised. This new-found wealth was used to speculate, especially by Berliners. With interest rates at only three per cent, there was no incentive to salt away the money in safety; instead, the Berlin Stock Exchange grew manically, with an increase in property development which hastened the growth of affluence and style. And the money just would not stop coming, for as profits increased to generate higher profits still, so profits increased speculation and vice versa in an upward spiral. The sparkle in the eye of this United Germany was Empire and industrial technology was the key to building that Empire, but to make any use at all of Imperial expansion, Germany also needed a strong deep-sea fleet, which could beat the competition in every field of maritime activity. Thereby hangs a tale, which started out as a mere whisper, but ended up as the factor which decided Britain's entry into war.

For a hundred years before the Treaty of Versailles, Great Britain had been developing the greatest deep-sea merchant fleet that the world has seen and was destined to retain that dominance for another hundred years. Without it, not a square yard of colonial soil would have been of any use, because there is no point in sweating over something if it is not going to benefit you in some way, and the only way in which the colonies could benefit the mother country, was by supplying commodities cheaply in order that the Imperial Capital could make a profit on it; and if there were no fleet to carry those commodities, the whole exercise would have been useless. As Britain discovered by experience, you had to have a navy which could protect that merchant fleet at all costs, against all enemies. And since the Battle of Trafalgar, no nation on Earth could contest the seas against the Royal Navy.

The story of empire-building has always been the same, and Germany well understood the vital importance of a world-beating maritime industry to its vision of Empire, both in terms of peaceful trade and wartime operations. German shipping companies took on a new significance for investment, Norddeutscher Lloyd building four giant superliners that outclassed all their British rivals on the North Atlantic, while equipping them with gun mountings that could make them formidable armed merchant cruisers if there were ever a war. Still, it was not enough; for the Kaiser had been encouraged to dream without limits, and the nation had been encouraged to dream in his image. Maybe he never saw the danger, or maybe he deluded himself with a dream of invincibility, but Wilhelm saw Berlin as the Challenger of London, and Germany as the new power that would humble the mighty British Empire – if only it could get the chance. Most of all, he dreamed of supremacy over the Royal Navy, Master of the High Seas for a hundred years, and such a victory would win Germany its avowed birth-right - put into words by Bulow when he addressed the Reichstag historically on the 6th December 1897, demanding that Germany, also, had a right to *a place in the sun*, with an empire of its own[4].

In truth, there were deeper national feelings against the British which flourished angrily in such an atmosphere, painting a much more sinister picture, and goes some way to explaining why the Germans' Hymn of Hate on the Western Front would focus on the British, rather than their long-established enemies, the French. Written shortly after the outbreak of war, it became immensely popular both at home and at the Front:

French and Russian, they matter not,
A blow for a blow and a shot for a shot!
We love them not, we hate them not,
We hold the Weichsel and Vosges gate......
We will never forego our hate,
We have all but a single hate,
We love as one, we hate as one,
We have one foe and one alone —
ENGLAND!

Dr Thomas Smith spent twelve years as English Lecturer at the University of Erlangen before taking his family back to England as the crisis broke on the last day of July 1914; in a remarkable monograph

---

[4] In fact, he had made the speech for very good political reasons, not to embark on a new age of Imperial Adventure (there was not much of the world left to make a profitable empire out of and, in any event, without the necessary maritime infrastructure, the venture would have been useless), but to head off a Conservative rebellion in the German parliament by telling them what they wanted to hear. It certainly worked, but the words are still remembered today, long after their real purpose has been forgotten.

of his observations of the German people he wrote that, while he harboured no animosity against his hosts, who treated him cordially, during at least eleven of those years he never wavered in his conviction that *Germans of all social classes look upon England as their inveterate enemy, and hate her... mixed with the hope that the day would come when England would be broken and humiliated*[5].

A historian may toil for a lifetime, to explain exactly how England engendered such vituperative abuse by ordinary German people. So far, they have achieved little success, save an idea that Britannia still ruled the waves which denied Germany its rightful Empire, and meant to keep it that way. Dr Smith was particularly struck by the spin that teachers gave to contemporary studies, in which England was portrayed as *a ruthless robber who from sheer motives of envy and lust of power has in turn smashed Holland, Spain and France.* Teachers hammered into their pupils that the writing was on the wall for Germany, which would become England's next target, because, as they saw it, Germany had come of age as England's commercial and naval rival. Rightly or wrongly, that rivalry had now matured.

An all-but fanatical disciple of Absolutism, Kaiser Wilhelm II was, however, dogged by such a deep-seated inferiority complex that it might be said to have been the root of his downfall - and the downfall of the world that he dragged into war. Looking back to those far-off times, it is difficult for us, today, to see clearly, and make out whether Germany followed his thinking, or whether he reflected German thinking but, we can be certain, that he believed that the Ancient Orders of Europe had deliberately encircled Germany to stifle its rightful ambition to join them and, as those European nations saw it,

---

[5] Smith, Dr T, 1915, The Soul of Germany: A Twelve Years Study of the People from Within, 1902-14, Grosset & Dunlap, New York

to lead them. Barbara Tuchman characterised the Kaiser with an irrational obsession that the other European Heads of State ignored him, and that they would not ignore him when the big guns of his new navy of ironclads roared. In reality, it was much more likely that the Heads of State distanced themselves from him as a man whom they disliked for his personal character, despite, even, their family ties. They were aware of his physical impairment with a withered arm but, perhaps, failed to understand the dreadful psychological consequences which that had on the man, and there was nobody who stood up to tell him the truth.[6]

It was just a question of time, before the Kaiser's dream would inevitably lead to war; by when the wave of 'New Imperialism', sweeping through the German middle and upper classes, had even left the German government lagging behind. By unhappy chance, it was reinforced by the steel of Clausewitz's philosophy, which waged war without compromise, who asserted that *War knows of only one method: force.* His words, which assumed positively biblical authority for the German State, conveyed with stark clarity that war must be to the death, destroying the enemy with brute force to the utmost. Lawyers may dictate their view of power that the State should be subservient to International Law but, observed Clausewitz, International Law is just a product of the modern world, and has no effect on the philosophy of war. Big Guns speak louder than International Law.

No more shocking example can be found than in August 1914, when the Germans razed the magnificent Belgian city of Louvain to the ground, in retaliation for what they perceived as civilian violation of the rules of war for attacking German combatants. Reprisals were savage; for five consecutive days the city was burned and looted, while

---

[6] Tuchman, B, 1962, The Guns of August, reprinted 2009 Random House

civilians were rounded up and executed, regardless of age or gender. It rapidly became clear that this was now a standard German strategy of intimidating occupied Belgian territory as a means of securing maximum civilian co-operation. A German officer, in charge of one street, said to the American First Secretary witnessing the holocaust *We shall wipe it out, not one stone will stand upon another. Not one I tell you. We will teach them to respect Germany. For generations people will come here to see what we have done.*

Well, actually, he was right. But not in the way he imagined.

THE BIRTH OF A DYNASTY

On the face of it, why should we be concerned about the fate of Otto Scholz, rather than any other German prisoner of war who died in captivity? First and foremost, we must wrestle with the human emotions in this story and draw our own conclusions on his fate. If we take away the humanity, though, we are left with another facet of the story, for then it is not the individual who speaks to us, so much as the Golden Age of Imperial Berlin, of which he is such a powerful symbol. By his birth he represented the hopes and aspirations of the values and the order of German society; by his death, he reflected the brutality of a war which brought the Golden Age to a terrible end.

You should have been there, in springtime, in Berlin's Golden Age as the nineteenth century was drawing to a close. The very heart of this young Empire, forged after the crowning glory of the Franco-Prussian War, beat proudly for the new Germany, whose affluence sparkled in the crystal chandeliers of every fine house and palace. For the capital of Empire, springtime in the era of 1890 meant not just a season, but a state of mind. It was here, in a very fine home just off the Tiergarten, at number 103 Potsdamer Straße, that there must have been much joy and celebration on Friday, the 21st March 1890, their beloved second child, Otto was born. In a very direct way indeed, the world of Otto Scholz paints the rise and terrible fall of Imperial Germany indelibly into the story of Netley Hospital, and the clash of philosophies, and ethics, that go to the heart of this book.

The proud father was Otto Franz August Scholz, a Doctor of Law and a leading figure in the life of Imperial Berlin. But his heritage called across the centuries, from the country around the Upper and Middle

Oder. In Polish it's *Slak*, to the Czechs it's *Slezko*, and to the Germans it is *Schlesien*, or Silesia, a region in Central Europe bursting with history. Most of it is now within the borders of Poland, but with a small part in the Czech Republic, and another small region, which only became part of Silesia in 1815, in Germany.

The origins of the Scholz family were cradled in this fair land of Silesia, and the ancient town of Niederschwedeldorf, south-west of Kreisstadt, formerly the fortress of Glatz. It was a graceful, green and pleasant land of rolling hills and fertile valleys, and in the middle of the highlands, was the Scholz estate. The earliest ancestor of whom we know was Michael Scholz the Elder, who was born in 1600 and lived all his 96 years there. His son had to lead the people through tough times indeed, for this was just a generation after the German civil wars of the Thirty Years War, which had reduced entire regions to destruction and bankrupted the protagonists. Silesia's Germanisation really culminated in 1740, when Frederick the Great saw his chance and seized the rich lands from Maria Theresa in the War of the Austrian Succession. As a result, Prussia acquired the provinces of Upper and Lower Silesia; if only the people were as easy to manage.

The rich fertility of the soil and the size of the estates had brought the dynastic families great wealth, and such comfort gave them the chance to acquire rich cultural values, with life-styles quite different from those of the poorer Junker families in other parts of eastern Germany; rather, they were more akin to the noble families of Poland. Theirs was a world which rejoiced in hunting, pitting their wits against the wild boar and wolves of the great forests, embracing a medieval idea of sportsmanship that was akin to the landed gentry of England. Here they indulged in extravagant balls, for they loved entertaining; as a well-known proverb ran, *when a guest enters the house, God enters also.* They also loved aristocratic intrigues; indeed, everything associated with European élite

society, in its way the Wagnerian ideal. It was not Utopian, though –
they had a great deal of affection for their peasants, but they flogged
them too. There was no crossing of the social boundaries to dilute the
blood of the nobility in those days, and the Scholz blood line was very
rich indeed. In the shadows, you can see the darkness of the Wagnerian
ideal.

The peaceful life which the Scholz forebears thought would last forever,
was broken with the footfalls of the army belonging to Napoleon
Bonaparte. The rigid and slow-moving Prussian army was no match
for the military genius of the Corsican Emperor, who destroyed it in
the twin battles of Jena and Auerstadt on the 14th October 1806. The
German families of Silesia watched the Prussian army fall back
helplessly and put their hopes in an advancing army of their allies,
Russia, to turn the invader back. The Russians never came. On the 19th
December 1806, Napoleon made his triumphant entry into Warsaw,
and the Grand Duchy of Warsaw gave the Polish people new hope of
nationhood. It was there that Count Krasinski received an audience
with the Emperor who gave him command of a dashing new regiment
of Polish lancers that made hearts beat a little bit faster. They did not
let him down, serving the Emperor at the time of his victorious
campaign in Silesia, during which he took the great fortress of Glatz,
close to the Scholz family estate. Everybody feared the Polish Uhlans;
but they admired them too.

The Polish dream did not last long, though and, when Napoleon's
Empire fell in 1815, Poland fell with it and its power was lost. It meant
that, now, the Scholz family could embrace the Germanic culture with
which they identified, and the Prussian province of Silesia was born. It
came at just the right time, as Germanic culture was blossoming with
the simple tastes of the Biedermeier era, striking just the right note with
a people who were recovering from war and occupation. More of a

mood than a style, it characterised the age fondly remembered as the cradle of Hoffmann, who created the *Nusskracker und Mauskönig*, the story of a Christmas gift for the children of a well-to-do family, with a sympathetic soul, and which inspired some of the greatest musical works ever composed. Closer, still, to the Scholz family seat, was a new literary genre that had been inspired when Mary Shelley visited nearby in 1814, and borrowed the town's name for her classic, *Frankenstein*, strangely echoing a legend of the work of some local undertakers in 1606.

Today, south-western Silesia is still a beautiful place, and from Niederschwedeldorf you can see the mountains covered with deep, mature forests, where in some places the snow lingers until late in the spring, sometimes until April. In June, on some mountain meadows, there blossoms a beautiful plant, which is unique to southern Silesia, and is known as the Glatzer rose, which covers the meadows of the Glatz mountainsides. Just as the edelweiss symbolises the Alps beloved of Bavaria in the south-west, so the Glatzer rose symbolises this beautiful mountain range in the north-east, where, you can imagine, the heroes of Wagner's works, beloved of the Prussian aristocracy, sleep peacefully in their dream-castles. What can compare in life with the feeling when you wake up in the early morning in winter, to be greeted by that strange, clear light, which seems to beckon impatiently through the shutters? That light which you only get when you open the frosty windows to gaze in wonder on a landscape of fresh snow, sparkling beneath a porcelain celestial blue sky, a snow-scene stretching as far as the eye can see, across the park, the lake, the ornate domes and spires of the churches glittering in the sunshine, to the endless, timeless forests beyond. Then it would be all furs and sleigh rides with your sweetheart, and such memories of hot glühwein in Christmas markets that nobody could ever forget.

Now we must be introduced to another great player on the stage of this drama, the other half of the dynasty which gave them the family name of Scholz-Forni. The ancestors of the Forni di Viano family could be traced back even further than the Scholzes – they were notable in 1230. On the 24th January 1801, the noble head of the house, Andrea Forni di Viano, died at his Italianate home in Breslau, where he had founded a trading house which the German poet Gustav Freytag used as his model for his novel *Debit and Credit*. The Forni di Viano family came from Lake Como, the most beautiful of all the lakes in the southern Alps, from where they spread their wings, and moved to Breslau with ambitions that won them power and glory in finance and politics. It was in 1813, that the family acquired one of the most beautiful stately homes in Europe, the Chateau of Glaesen-Steubendorf, the very epitome of a romantic lodge.

Here in Silesia, the Scholz and the Forni families met and married; the blood proved a good mix, and a dynasty was born[7], alongside those of many of the great names in Prussia's story; the Ministers von Duseberg and von Muhler, the big Mecklenburg landowners, Diestel and Stamer, the Hamburg trading families Amsinck and Woermann, were all known, and all were welcome friends to the Scholz family in those gloriously young years of the Germanic Confederation. They were glorious, as mighty energies were generated in the power-house of those influential families whom the Scholz and Forni families knew so well, and set to work in the new age of enterprise which would bring untold prosperity for Germany in the nineteenth century, that would pay for their industrialisation – and, ultimately, their downfall.

---

[7] History of the Scholz family *passim*, Scholz-Forni, R, 1941, Die Scholz-Forni und ihre Anverwandten, Hamburg

THE WORLD OF OTTO SCHOLZ

Otto Franz August Scholz was an Imperial Berliner. While Silesia might have inspired a composer to write a musical Souvenir, the life of court and salon in Imperial Berlin had inevitably drawn the family there with something much more powerful. He was born there, and baptised on the 12th August 1847, according to the rites of the Catholic church, in the beautiful *Rundkeppelbau* by the State Opera House. His godparents were the Finance Minister, Franz von Duesberg, the Appeal judge and later Head of the State Tribunal, Otto Forni, as well as the wife of Minister von Muhler and President Busse.

He was a gifted student, and at 22 years old was awarded a Doctorate in Law; but in 1870 the Franco-Prussian war broke out and he was gazetted to the 12th Company of the Guard-Fusilier Regiment, where he was appointed to the Staff of General Witten. The war clouds passed, of course and he was anxious to return to his career in the law, which would take him on a meteoric rise, that led him to Hannover in 1879, where he met a delightful debutante, Amelie Diestel. He wrote about his new lady, *she is a lovely little creature*, and, on the 8th May 1885, he married Amelie at Gross-Brutz, in Mecklenburg. But amidst this beautiful picture of sophisticated charm and happiness, the gods had capriciously painted in a terrible, fatal flaw, for Amelie had an incurable mental health disease, inherited from her family and which she would pass on to her youngest son. We do not know how that was diagnosed, particularly as psychiatry was all but unknown at that time. Even today, the diagnosis of mental illness is not fully understood, nor how it can be inherited.

Amid this life of influence, culture and style, on the 21st March 1890, their beloved second child, Otto Paul Carl, was born in Berlin. He had an older brother, Robert, who had been born in 1886 and a younger sister, Amelie, who was born in 1896. Their mother was a good mother, loving and strong for them and their father. She understood the importance of keeping the family close, playing with the children herself and organising charming little fetes for them, instead of leaving them to the governess, as so many mothers of her class used to do. Of course, the magic of Christmas was the highlight of their year, which the whole entertainment of *Weihnachten* brings carolling and folk tradition into harmony with the German soul, and nobody could organise a Christmas as special or as magical as Amelie did. Robert remembered all his life, that Christmas when he was seven years old, dressing up as a little *Weihnachtsmann*, a traditional Christmas character, reciting a delightful poem so redolent of the values of Home and Family at Christmas. It tells us about something deep in the German soul that never goes away, and was found even in the trenches of 1914.

The children's father had been going from strength to strength. His intellect stood him in good stead, when he won the much sought-after position of Senator in Berlin. He had a veritable army of civil servants to assist him, but he was too wise to put all his faith in the advice of those who might have had political ambitions of their own, and was guided by his wife, Amelie. Her mental health was gradually growing more delicate, though and the family's private history put it in an understandably euphemistic way, that her health was becoming a growing worry for her devoted husband. By the time of Otto's birth, his father had already been appointed the Chief Justice of the Province of Brandenburg, and was now 43 years old. To look at his picture, one sees a stern man, every inch a Prussian, and he lived up to the ideal; Robert remembered his father's moral torch that *Youth is not there to amuse them, but to prepare them for their situation in life.* Yet, he instilled great love and affection in his younger son, Otto, as we shall see.

By the time that Otto was celebrating his twenty-second birthday in 1912, Berlin had reached its zenith, with a budget of 350 million marks a year. But it had also undergone a political revolution, with the Socialists outnumbering everybody else in the Parliament.

Young Otto studied at the Prinz-Heinrich Gymnasium in Berlin; like his father, he was an outstandingly good scholar, and in the acid test of his school-leaving examination, he shone both in his written and oral work. The discipline of Otto's childhood was harsh, but it bred in the teenager a self-confidence, a belief in oneself and the Fatherland, as Otto mapped out his plans for a career in the Prussian Higher Civil Service. Such a position was one of the accepted courses for the professional aristocracy, the *Briefadel,* and against the background of Imperial Germany, we can now paint in our portrait of Otto, on course for that exclusive calling. He qualified handsomely to study at Freiburg im Breslau, in their ancient family homeland of Silesia, before progressing to the distinguished school of Law and State Sciences in Berlin.

Otto's elder brother, Robert, had chosen a military career and, upon being admitted to the German Officer Corps, he joined Field Artillery Regiment (Prince-Regent Luitpold of Bavaria) No 4. They were equipped with light howitzers, powerful, lethal weapons that could be moved rapidly in the heat of battle to the place where they could have the deadliest effect on the enemy. The artillery was not the noblest branch of the forces - that was the cavalry - but it was the home of the real professionals in the Army. And the High Command knew it, for it was the artillery that enjoyed the highest investment in the whole German Army.

In the winter of 1908, Otto wrote a letter to his brother, who was then a *Leutnant* serving with his Regiment at Magdeburg. By that time, already, their mother's health had become a worry, and Otto asked after her. His brother recalled in the family history how the letter revealed that Otto was enjoying the student life in which, as part of his rite of passage, he had joined the *Freikorps*, which was unquestionably a fine and noble thing for students of his Class to aspire to, and he was proud of the nickname which his fellow-students had bestowed upon him: the Fox. He had made the first team in fencing, and was immensely proud of his duelling scar, which, he wrote, *is healing well, so tomorrow I can fence again.* Here was a young Prussian lion, if ever there was one. His studies were pressing, though, and would not be denied.

On the 8th December 1911, Otto passed the first examination of the King's Law Chambers with a good assessment, so that, on the 6th January following, he was able to progress to his first Candidacy as a Lawyer in the Prussian Higher Civil Service. Yet, Otto's professional plans came hand-in-hand with the demands of society's protocol for a commission in the Officer Reserve. It was this which enabled a young man to combine a professional career or management of the family estate with a position in that most respected - and indispensable - of Prussian institutions, the Army. Membership of the gilt-edged club of the Officer Reserve was an essential status symbol at the top of the complex Prussian social system, a feudal society unashamedly dominated by the Army - and the dream of every dashing young man was a commission in the light cavalry. Such a position reflected the holder's status at the top of the class.

In peace-time, every German male aged between 17 and 45 was eligible for military service, which lasted three years in the cavalry; but such a dry statement undervalues the enormous part which a military listing for a person played in Berlin society. In the cavalry Regiments not a single bourgeois name could be found among the regular officers, but they could boast 34 princes and 51 counts. Leadership of the profession of arms for generations had been the exclusive preserve of the hereditary nobility, who were thus able to hold on to their unrivalled domination of society. In 1814, universal military training was introduced, which meant that, for the rising educated middle classes, the Reserve Officer Corps was born and, while such a social background precluded a regular commission in the top Regiments, membership of the Reserve provided that vital key for the new middle classes which opened the door to the top of Prussian social acceptability.

So, for all Otto's intellectual ambitions as a lawyer in the Higher Civil Service, his military service had to be pursued, as well. There were circumstances in which the three-year period of military service could be abbreviated, enabling privileged and gifted young men to serve just one year as *Einjahrig-Freiwilliger*; moreover, they were permitted to choose which Regiment they would join, rather than have a posting allocated to them. The 2nd Hannover Dragoon Regiment, Number 16 in the German Army's consolidated list, was a cavalry Regiment whose Colonel in Chief was King Albert of Belgium – just another of Europe's plethora of monarchs, one might think, but, in fact, he was about to demonstrate bravery that set him above all the other crowned heads of the time.

Maybe, it had been a posting which had been secured by his father's influence, for Otto (Senior) had powerful contacts in Hannover. From the winter of 1912 to October 1913, Otto spent his required year as *Einjahrig-Freiwilliger* with the 16th Dragoons, based in the beautiful old city of Lüneburg, where he served with his friend, the son of Minister von Sydow, sharing a batman with several other one-year volunteers. While most of the Regiment would mess in the garrison, the *Einjahrig-Freiwilliger* usually dined at a restaurant in town. Together, they learned the meaning of leadership as potential officers, and could rise to the effective rank of sergeant. Usually, the one-year volunteer would then graduate to the Reserve service as a *Vizewachtmeister*, or Squadron Sergeant Major, until qualifying for a commission.

Had Otto's career followed the plans which he had cherished, he would have been able to concentrate on his professional career, and carve a name for himself in the law, as had his father, and his grandfather before him. But only months more were left to him, before Europe went to war. At last, following the completion of his year's service, he was able to progress his law career and applied for, and was granted, the coveted position of *Regierungsreferendar*, a candidacy in the Higher Civil Service with the Government, when he was appointed to Frankfurt am Oder, in the Prussian Provincial Administration. Now, on the brink of hostilities, Otto had to turn from his career, to face his responsibilities to his home and his Fatherland. We have seen how peace-time routine would have required that he serve with the rank of *Vizewachtmeister* before his name finally came up before the officers of the Regiment, who would vote that he should, indeed, join the noble ranks of the Officer Corps. Time had run out for peace-time routine, though. Now he was commissioned as a *Leutnant Der Reserve* in the Officer Corps; but a nobler Regiment, still, awaited him.

The von Linsingens were one of those old army families that fortified the fabric of the Hannoverian aristocracy, and they had reached the pinnacle of their power. Alexander von Linsingen had joined the Prussian army 46 years previously and now commanded II Corps of the German First Army. Another von Linsingen, however, had been promoted to Lieutenant Colonel in October 1913, and now commanded one of the finest regiments in the German army – the regiment which Otto was now to join, almost entirely thanks to his family's influence. Its full title said something of that pride:

PREUßISCHEN ULANENREGIMENT "KAISER ALEXANDER II VON RUßLAND" (1 BRANDENBURGISCHEN) Nr 3.

The 3rd Uhlans were a Regiment of lancers, raised in the reflected glory of the magnificent Polish light cavalry who had been led by Count Krasinski in the service of Napoleon, and Europe never quite forgot them. Lancers were the most fearless - and the most feared - sort of light cavalry that had originated centuries before in the armies of the Cossacks (Uhlan is an old Tatar word for a noble commander). However nervous the Polish horsemen may have made their German neighbours on the Scholz estate in Silesia, they certainly cut a dash in Napoleon's Army and, in the great battles in which they played such a strong part, these outstanding horsemen, armed with their national weapon, the lance, impressed all of Europe, so that in Prussia, Regiments of lancers were raised, modelled on the Polish pattern. One of these was the 3rd, raised in 1809, which formed part of the new Prussian Army that metamorphosed in the wake of the trouncing inflicted by Napoleon at Jena and Auerstadt in October 1806. It was not so long before Prussian and Russian were fighting shoulder to shoulder against Napoleon's battle-hardened Army in their determination to rid themselves of the Thief of Europe.[8]

Russia would not forget the 3rd Uhlans. On the 12th June 1829, King Friedrich Wilhelm II of Prussia was pleased to appoint the heir to the Russian throne to be the Honorary Colonel of the Regiment. When he

---

[8] When the Prussian forces finally reached the British lines to turn the tide at the Battle of Waterloo on the 18th June 1815, it was said that the last sound of battle in the Napoleonic Age was the trumpet call of a Polish lancer, covering the Emperor's (short-lived) escape.

became Tsar of all the Russias in 1855, the Prussian cabinet decreed that the Regiment should be called after him, *Kaiser Alexander II von Rußland*, and they were permitted the distinction of wearing his monogram on their epaulettes[9]. By the turn of the century, the regimental standard was festooned with honours bestowed by the royal houses of both Prussia and Russia, while the Regiment had another Colonel-in-Chief from Russia, Grand Duke Serge Alexandrovich Romanov, the fifth son of Alexander II and a controversial figure who, when Governor of Moscow in 1892, had the city's Jewish quarter sacked by Cossacks and the residents, mostly artists and merchants, ruthlessly thrown out. Horrifyingly, the Tsar had no problem with this – such things come with the job description when you are an autocrat.[10]

Today, a century since the guns fell silent, progress has long since wiped away the memory of that indefinable blend of pulse-quickening excitement and romance which we can hardly begin to imagine. Yet this was the life-blood of the 3rd Uhlans and their ladies as they waltzed to the music of Strauss beneath crystal chandeliers at sumptuous balls, dancing the night away. Actually they had to dance the night away, because it was a matter of honour that officers should take part in every dance of the evening; but of course they still had a lot of time to toast the ladies, the Fatherland and, of course, each other.

Equally, there would have been grand military spectacles as proud old men and young sweethearts watched the 3rd Uhlans parade to the jaunty, devil-may-care strains of their Regimental march, the *Kaiser Alexander Ulanen-Marsch*, lance pennants fluttering, horses prancing

---

[9] After his death, the Regiment kept the honour in its title; such a distinction is not to be discarded lightly.

[10] The 3rd Uhlans would not have Grand Duke Serge as its Colonel-in-Chief for long, though, for in 1905 he was assassinated by a terrorist bomb while leaving the Kremlin in his carriage – a haunting repetition of his father's fate.

spiritedly, as they honoured, God, Kaiser and Fatherland; but especially, the brotherhood of their Regiment. All in the Regiment, from the newest recruit to Colonel von Linsingen, took a pride in the uniform, which the soldiers wore constantly, and the Uhlan was distinctive in his tunic with a broad, double-breasted front, piped in scarlet. It was a light, easy-fitting uniform, with - to the envy of the British cavalry (who wore puttees and cords) - loose trousers reinforced for riding with soft black leather, and soft leather boots level with the knee. What really marked the Uhlan out from the crowd, though, was the traditional lancer's head-dress. Somehow retaining its ancient name of *Tschapka*, its distinctive 'mortar-board' on the crown outwardly looked a little bizarre but, in fact, was extremely functional, for it very effectively deflected glancing sword-blows to the head.

The Regimental History contains photographs of some of Otto's comrades among the Officer Corps in the 3rd Uhlans – the face of *Oberleutnant* Freiherr von Reiswiß und Kanderzin belongs to a young man who is intelligent and sensitive, while *Rittmeister* (Captain) von Kuhne, an officer in the Reserve like Otto, has a deep wound or, possibly, a duelling scar above his right eye, and a light moustache with close-cropped beard that would become all the rage in the twenty first century. *Rittmeister* von Roeder looks hardened, much more grave, wrapped up in a fur-lined coat, and standing with a stick that speaks of a battlefield wound – and well it might, for he would always lead from the front, as we shall see. But to the last man, their bearing speaks more eloquently of the style of a Kaiser's Uhlan than mere words can convey, emphasising the pride and the supreme self-confidence of an Uhlan of the Imperial German Army. There was no doubt about it, the 3rd Uhlans had style[11].

The Uhlans had a cutting edge to all this. The job of the light cavalry

---

[11] von Stranß was killed in December 1914, and von Dittmar in 1918.

was primarily reconnaissance, specialising in intelligence-gathering and skirmishing, riding ahead of his advancing Army, probing the enemy, discovering their strengths and weaknesses and reporting back to headquarters; the Uhlan was, indeed, the eyes and the ears of the generals. But the Uhlan had teeth as well. Armed with a lance 10 feet 6 inches long, a sword and a Mauser carbine, he rode a horse as fast as a fury, that jumped like a stag and turned like a polo pony - in fact, he had probably been with that same horse for both of their military careers, so horse and man were as one. In short, the Uhlan could get out of trouble as fast as he got into it.

Officers were armed with a sword - an ancient weapon yet still indispensable when having to cut yourself out of a tight close-quarters situation - and a Luger automatic pistol, one of the most highly prized firearms carried by any side during the war. Georg Luger's design had been perfected in 1908, with a lug attached to the heel of the pistol frame for attachment of a shoulder stock, turning it into a light and lethal carbine as the need arose. It fired a 9 millimetre bore cartridge, containing a 123-grain truncated-nose bullet that was intended to increase the wounding effect of the fully-jacketed bullet. Over two million Luger pistols were used by German forces from 1914 to 1918, and they had absolute confidence in it as they went about their work. The Uhlan officer had to have daring and initiative, a keen eye and complete knowledge of his craft. He had a swagger in his step and a panache in his salute, but then he had to carry out his job with deadly coolness in a crisis when what the mind really wanted to do was panic[12].

A glance at the Officers' List for the 3rd Uhlans reveals their

---

[12] For further information on the organisation and armament of the Imperial German Army see Cron, H, 2006, Imperial German Army 1914-1918, Helion & Co, Solihull, Marrion, R, 1975, Lancers and Dragoons: Uniforms of the Imperial German Army, Almark, Nash, D, 1918, Handbook of the Imperial German Army 1914-1918, Ian Allan

distinguished part in the society of East Prussia - and the same names keep appearing, generation after generation. The Officer Corps recruited among the sons and grandsons of serving and former officers of the Regiment as well as from the landed gentry. Everybody lived up to the same creed, that service to the Fatherland was the top vocation, worth more than all the worldly goods that money could buy. On top of that, it was the foundation of good comradeship. No doubt this *esprit de corps* contributed to the headstrong enthusiasm of so many of the young officers, freshly graduated from the Cadet Corps or from War School, when the order was heard on the training field, *Trumpeter, sound the Gallop*; inevitably you would soon hear some veteran's voice calling out, *Herr Leutnant, get back behind the front line!*

An excellent corps of Non-Commissioned Officers formed the backbone of the 3rd Uhlans, especially the veteran regulars, the sergeants, such as Richter, who had joined up in 1891, Schreck in 1894 and Deutschmann in 1898. These men had seen *everything*, they knew what made the Regiment tick and would play their part far beyond the call of duty in the coming war. One or two would survive the carnage of the early years and get commissioned - valuable officers, indeed. The troopers were almost exclusively young men who had come from the countryside, strong, healthy lads who had volunteered to join through their love for horses. It was a 'Happy Regiment', in which everybody shared a bond, a mutual belief in themselves and in each other, something quite indefinable and which they learned and fostered without being told about it; perhaps it is this mutual belief and understanding, which makes a 'Happy Regiment', be it a Prussian Uhlan, a British Dragoon or a Russian Cossack.

Otto's own family, with its aristocratic roots in the East Prussian mountains of Silesia, had its own part to play; even though they were not Princes, or Counts, or even 'vons', they shared the society of the noblest and most ancient dynasties. Consider, for a moment, the Officers of the Reserve in the Regiment, whose names speak of ancient origins in the wild fastnesses of Europe, such as von Schenk zu Tautenburg, von Kottwiss, and von Wallenberg-Pachaln. Most famously of all, *Leutnant* von Jagow, was a troop leader in the 1st Squadron; he came from the same family as the German Foreign Secretary, Gottlieb von Jagow, who, with the Chancellor, Theobold von Bethman Hollweg, steered German foreign policy in the years leading up to the war. That crucially important social position as an Officer in the Reserve served them well, while serving in the Prussian Government Service, or looking after their estates in a picture of gracious society that was swept away forever by war and revolution, before the twentieth century reached its age of majority. What is inescapable, is that it was the normative ethics of the society which bred such people, that defined the structure of the German war machine, and which led to 636 burials in the cemetery at Netley Hospital. So just what was inside the skin of the Uhlan?

As a Prussian officer, Otto was allowed to use his own individual initiative to a greater degree than his counterpart in the British Army; indeed, to Lieutenant Osmond Williams of the British 19th Hussars, who reported to the General Staff in January 1907, *the average German officer seems to look upon soldiering in a more serious light than the British officer does*. The downside to the Prussian military system, was in the ranks. Discipline in the ranks was perfect, indeed, Williams thought that, sometimes it was too strict, to the point of smothering any individual initiative. In the British Army, things were different; while the officers were not so professionally committed and independent thinking frowned upon, the NCO's and men in this totally volunteer Army were able to demonstrate the individual initiative which had become the trademark of the Tommy in combat; crucially, it would make the difference between defeat and victory in 1914, when officers were wiped out, and troops made it back under the command of sergeants, corporals - even privates.

On the whole, though, Williams was mightily impressed with the German cavalry, and compared them surprisingly favourably with the British. He was especially impressed with the *greatest keenness* that was displayed in the result of an inspection - even that of a Squadron. Every officer of the Regiment had to be present, whether or not he belonged to the Squadron that was being inspected. Everyone took the greatest interest, and great was the discussion which took place at its close as to the respective merits of the various Squadrons. As a result, there was intense, but friendly and very healthy, rivalry.

The German officer was always in uniform, and so there was a splendid show at every race meeting, where German officers were able to show off their horsemanship as well as their sporting skills. Surprisingly, though, hunting was rare, and polo was not allowed at all. Indulgence in sports that lacked the feudal ideals of the Officer Corps weakened the Teutonic system.

In Otto's Squadron, the 4th Squadron, there were three other officers, 163 other ranks and 178 horses. Four vehicles were on the Squadron strength as well, a sign of the times indeed. Three more Squadrons of lancers and a machine gun Squadron made up the fighting strength of the Regiment. Their home was at Fürstenwalde, east of Berlin. Every German Regiment had its own headquarters, and it never moved except under exceptional circumstances. From the point of view of training and organisation generally, it was an enormous advantage, forming strong local bonds, but most importantly, all horses trained in the Regiment remained with its troopers, sometimes as long as twelve or fifteen years - the whole of their working lives. The bonds that grew up between man and horse can be well-imagined; by contrast, when a British Regiment was transferred from one station to another, as it always was, the horses were left behind for the incoming Regiment.

Each German Squadron received its quota of 40 recruits on a fixed date each year, when the men underwent a six-months recruits' course before they took their places in the ranks. In this manner, every recruit had an equal amount of training. They were, of course, conscripts, but Williams noted an advantage even in this; because of the conscription process they were drawn from every class, with the result that the average German recruit was better educated than his counterpart in the British Army. Where they fell down, was in their veterinary knowledge, with regard to wounds, lameness, and the conformation of the horse generally, although Williams observed, *the way they look and turn out their horses leaves nothing to be desired.*

Annually, on the 1st July, every Squadron received 15 remounts. A Squadron leader was very much in the same position as an owner of a large hunting, or racing stable, with his troop leaders as stud grooms. He could sell or buy horses as he saw best; so long as he turned out his correct complement on parade, he was given absolutely a free hand. He constantly had his remounts under his own eye, so he was able to follow their progress and learn each horse's peculiarities. This was where so much advantage was gained by being based permanently on one station, so the Squadron kept the horses they trained and nurtured throughout their working lives.

Williams cast an expert eye over the horses:

The horses seem to be at least three parts thoroughbred, with a touch of Arab. Perhaps they are a little light boned compared with our horses. Well-bred bone, however, although perhaps a shade small, is better than big bone that is coarse. One noteworthy thing in the horses is the prevailing lightness of mouth, and the men seem to be able to do anything with them.

It was just as well, because the trooper could hardly ever use both hands to control his horse, as he was encumbered with his lance, an ancient weapon that was inferior, even, to its counterpart in the British Army, which was much lighter, made of bamboo. As a result of the difficulties in control, the Uhlan rode at a much slower pace than his enemy, for control was better maintained when travelling more slowly, and he usually circled round each 'point' before thrusting. In order to compensate for the limited control, great emphasis was placed on the obedience of leg and rein, every day, before drill, the men having to ride their horses at a very slow and collected canter.

That being said, the paces of the horse were perfect, especially the 'amble', a huge advantage in long-distance marches which was unknown in the British Army. Every horse moved with a long, easy stride, always perfectly quiet and never, under any circumstances taking anything out of himself.

The remounts were trained by the best riders in the Squadron. The Squadron leader was able to study the progress of his men at the same time as that of the horses, and good riders would always come to the fore. They were necessarily NCOs, since few troopers could become good horsemen in their two-years' conscription service. A ride of young horses was therefore nearly always composed of sergeants and corporals, under an officer or Squadron Sergeant-major. Remount training was carried out under Squadron supervision and the German officer made the most of his ample time to train his young horses - and in the process, of course, Squadron officers themselves learned the way to set about training young horses. The competitive element between Squadrons meant that each Squadron officer would try to get his horses more efficiently and quickly trained than those of other Squadrons.

The crux of the daily routine was centred, of course, on the horse. Each Squadron had its own stables, with hay loft containing the animals' feed, and always kept in a condition to beat its rivals. At the foot of each stall hung a board which gave the horse's name and date of joining. Each year had a different letter and all remounts in that year would have names beginning with that letter; on the face of it, this was perhaps a rather tedious show of German order, but it had a useful purpose, because in this way a horse's name was sufficient to tell his date of joining and approximate age. Black duty boards hung in each stable with printed headings, giving the names of those horses for the day's duties, the number of sick horses, and hour of parade.

The bedding in the stalls consisted of an excellent quality of straw, always kept down and mucked out morning and evening, while the animals were fed on 10 lbs of corn a day and about 14 of hay; in addition, they received a daily feed of chaff, usually damped and mixed with oats at each feed.

The Uhlan mounted up into a saddle that he believed was much better than his enemy's, with knee rolls and light papier maché panels, secured with string girths that lasted an age longer than the British Army's webbing. The seat was believed to be much better-shaped and, when the rider sat into it, the flexible saddle bent to the shape of almost any sort of back. All the training and manoeuvres had failed to expose its major defect, though: it could not stand the wear and tear of a prolonged campaign in all weathers. The bridle was sensibly designed, though, with practically a double bridle, except that the cheeks of the bit, instead of being rounded, were flatter.

Out on manoeuvres, the Uhlan held his lance in his right hand, and his sword was carried on the opposite, or near-side, while his carbine was carried on the off-side in a leather bucket, with a flap which fastened around the small of the butt. It all seemed very neat and tidy, but when the fighting got hot, and a few moments could mean the difference between life and death, the trooper would find this a disadvantage. The crux would come when they were forced to fight dismounted; it was something which the Germans tended to ignore, and gave the troopers precious little shooting practice, while the British placed great emphasis on it, and the baptism of August and September 1914 proved how priceless it was to be. Williams drew the picture:

German cavalry do not believe much in dismounted work. Nearly everyone is thoroughly opposed to getting off his horse more often than is necessary; they take longer to do so than the British, anyway. If the led horses need moving, odd numbers must remain mounted so as to carry the lances of those in the firing line. This diminishes their strength as compared to our "no 3" system [one man holds the horses for himself and two comrades who are then free to combat the enemy]. In an emergency, it is some time before the men commence firing, as handing over the lance, unstrapping the carbine flap forming up, commanded right or left turn and extending takes time. They then throw themselves down on their stomachs, but troop leaders have to shout out the distance of the object fired at, and the men seem very careful in fixing their sights.

While mass cavalry tactics were discouraged, emphasis was placed on shock action in small groups at troop or Squadron strength, when the Uhlan's lance was at its most useful. When the order to charge was given, the men started their horses into a charge-gallop from a fairly slow canter; so, the perfectly-trained men and horses were still fresh on striking the enemy. A great deal of jumping in line was practised, and only once did Lieutenant Williams see a horse refuse. Ditches and mud walls boarded on the top were generally used, placed in different parts of the drill ground, which was a big, soft, sandy flat about 2 miles by 1 mile.

Williams was mightily impressed by what he saw of German cavalry, particularly when he watched them at the Charge:

To see a German Squadron charge, no doubt can be left in anyone's mind as to the superiority of the lance in this particular class of work. A Squadron which is unprovided with this weapon, could not stand up against a frontal charge by one which is so provided.

Perhaps, though, Williams was just a little over-impressed by what he saw. As a weapon, the lance had real advantages in open country, against enemy cavalry as well as at close quarters scraps with foot soldiers, provided that the soldiers were standing up, smartly advancing in line. But when they were in extended order, taking cover, lying flat on the ground or rooted in trenches, the lance was a useless piece of equipment, and there was little value to be had with a lance when confronted with machine guns and high-velocity rifles. All the pros and cons had seen the demise of the lance as early as the American Civil War. Williams subsequently brought himself back down to earth, when he qualified his opinion:

There are, of course, serious and very obvious objections to the use of the lance, and it is doubtless a consideration of these which has caused their practical disappearance from our service.

The drill ground was the trooper's second home. Here, the Squadron leaders spared no pains to bring their men to perfection, at first moving slowly, and then gradually increasing the pace as time went on, taking their Squadrons at the 'march past' six or seven times at the one pace until they got it absolutely perfect: 48 men in the front rank, 30 to 40 in the rear rank. All movements in line, especially getting into that formation, were particularly important, before moving off to a flank in line at the gallop. And the horses knew as much about the drill as the younger men, due to the excellence of their training.

One of the things which struck Williams most compellingly, was the cavalry's constant cheering:

On a German cavalry training ground shouts and cheers are heard coming from every quarter. At first it gives the impression that someone has been badly hurt. Sections, troops, Squadrons, and Regiments are always practising this shouting. Even men at lance exercise often keep up a continual "hurrah, hurrah" from start to finish. The object appears to be to accustom the horses to the sudden volume of sound, so that in war they will not get out of hand.

Perhaps, as well, it had a huge effect on morale, while equally demoralising the poor bloody infantry whom the Uhlans were charging towards at that moment.

THE PATH TO HELL

We can look at the deepening crisis between the nations from the British or the German viewpoint; but that does not help us to understand how the likes of Otto's generation across Europe watched them all stumbling down this path, which ended up in Hell. We need to pause for a moment, and watch the events build up to war.

History never does things in isolation, so when we see a faded photograph of Great War patients at Netley Hospital, we have to understand the path that led them there. When Bülow declared, in 1897, that Germany had a legitimate demand to *a Place in the Sun*, he may have appeased the Conservatives in the Reichstag, but it was a rash juggling of priorities, for he started the first roll of a snowball, which would loom ever larger in the fears of the European Imperial Capitals. It was abundantly clear to them all, as much to any schoolboy studying a map of the world, that there was no new territory left to conquer and carve out for an Imperial possession. It meant that, if Germany meant to have its Place in the Sun, it would have to seize possessions from France, or Britain.

From the viewpoint of Otto's contemporaries in Paris and London, as the first decade of the twentieth century waned it looked like Germany was gearing up for the long-awaited new war that would engulf Europe; well, that was what they were told, and they believed it. They could also see that Berlin was becoming diplomatically isolated for it, which was no bad thing in French eyes, who were keen to fight back for Alsace-Lorraine, but the British were troubled, because isolation is the foundation stone of paranoia, which if unchecked only makes the prospect of war greater. But now was no time for appeasement; the

Allies had to start making plans for military co-operation that would emerge as the British Expeditionary Force.

It was when Berliners read the newspapers in 1911 that they realised that their ancient blood-family in England were going to betray them and, instead, support France, which had been the bitter enemy of both powers for so long. They read how the Chancellor of the Exchequer, David Lloyd George, rose to his feet at the Mansion House on the 21st July to deliver a stern warning against further German expansion:

I believe it is essential in the highest interests, not merely of this country, but of the world, that Britain should at all hazards maintain her place and her prestige amongst the Great Powers of the world.... National honour is no party question. The security of our great international trade is no party question; the peace of the world is much more likely to be secured if all nations realize fairly what the conditions of peace must be....[13]

The reaction to this speech electrified the chanceries of Europe: Paris was elated, while, in Berlin, the people were shocked and dismayed, with its very clear message that, in a European war between France and Germany, Great Britain would not sit on her hands, but would support the old adversary of both countries.

In the salons and the street cafés of Imperial Berlin, people felt let down - even betrayed - by Britain's avowed position against them, which, perhaps, explains why, in the forthcoming Great War, the entire German psyche presented a united front of hatred against Britain which far outstripped their hostility to France. In the early months of the war, Germans at home and at the Front were exhorted daily to recite, in something approaching a religious liturgy, the Hymn of Hate

---

[13] The Original can be accessed via www.lib.byu.edu/index.php/Agadir_Crisis:_ Lloyd_George's_Mansion_House_Speech

against the treacherous British of which we have spoken earlier. It ended thus:

You we will hate with a lasting hate,
We will never forego our hate,
Hate by water and hate by land,
Hate of the head and hate of the hand,
Hate of the hammer and hate of the crown,
Hate of seventy millions choking down.
We love as one, we hate as one,
We have one foe and one alone--
ENGLAND!

In truth, though, nobody was under any illusions about a long-term peace in Europe any more, and it became essential to perfect the plans for the British Expeditionary Force.

The powder kegs were being stacked up beneath the glorious *Belle Epoch* of European civilisation, that was absolutely dependent upon peace; ironically, the fuse to set them off came from a very different quarter. It had all started in the Balkans, the most unstable part of Europe, and the point of contact where three hostile empires met - Russia, Austria-Hungary, and the Ottomans. The break-up of the Ottoman Empire had been taking place for much of the nineteenth century, and its dismemberment left a vacuum which, inevitably, bred new tensions in the region.

Austria-Hungary was at the centre of the problem, really, the dying vestige of the Holy Roman Empire, which saw itself as the ancient defender of Christian civilisation against Turkish barbarism. As the Ottomans relaxed their grip on Serbia, Romania and Bulgaria, the peoples of Western Europe started reading in their newspapers about tensions in the Balkans. When Austria-Hungary then seized Bosnia for itself, nobody was really under any illusions about this ancient, two-crowned empire, which was seen as undemocratic and repressive to the brave new world to which little Bosnia aspired. And the fear spread - to Bosnia's Slavic brothers.

British history books do not dwell much upon the First Balkan War, which erupted in August 1912, but in Berlin it was a very different matter, breaking down the status quo in the Balkans and precipitated ever-worsening clashes between Russia and Austria-Hungary. Germany was right in the middle politically, and in very real terms the Silesia of the Scholz family estates were in the middle geographically. The peace negotiations that brought the First Balkan War to a close on the 30th May 1913 brought little respite, for the second war flared up on the night of the 29th – 30th June, when King Ferdinand of Bulgaria ordered his troops to attack Greek and Serbian positions. The Serbs, Greeks and Romanians routed the Bulgarians in such a successful campaign that, in just three weeks, the Bulgarian forces collapsed.

The Peace of Bucharest in August 1913 brought Serbia new lands (not received in Vienna with rejoicing) but the re-drawing of the borders required that she evacuate Albanian territory. Not only did Serbia not evacuate the land, but actually occupied still more land. For Austria-Hungary, this posed the problem that Serbia was beginning to threaten the dominance of the Habsburg dynasty. It is, perhaps, ironic that this dynasty was dying, and the Emperor-in-waiting, Franz Ferdinand, had already planned for a new democracy upon his accession, which surely could not be long in the future.

A warning to Belgrade from Vienna on the 1st October brought an evasive response: the pan-Slavic consciousness of Serbia was becoming a challenge now. Vienna sent an ultimatum on the 18th October: if Serbia did not leave Albanian soil within eight days, Austria-Hungary would have to resort to *proper means to assure the realisation of its demands*. On the very knife-edge of brinkmanship, Serbia backed down. But the tensions in the Balkans were becoming uncontainable; if Austro-Hungarian influence were to dominate, Habsburg policy towards Serbia now had to shift from constraint to combat.

It was this decision which would have such far-reaching consequences for the world, when the deadly serious diplomatic dancing in the Courts of Europe became so complicated, that the dynasties found themselves building an enormously complex powder keg of political confrontations, which needed just one spark to light the fuse, which would start a chain reaction that nobody could stop. The spark flashed in the Balkans, in a row that Berlin found itself dragged into, being shackled to Vienna, but could not do anything to stop.

On the 28th June 1914, Archduke Franz Ferdinand was visiting Sarajevo in Bosnia on an official visit - ill-advisedly, it had been chosen to coincide with Bosnia's National Day. God had, in fact, singled out Franz Ferdinand to be heir to the Austro-Hungarian Empire in preference to a remarkable number of better-placed contenders in the line of succession, and God had been very creative in the manner in which He had despatched them, taking the now middle-aged man to the front of the queue. First heir to the Emperor Franz Joseph was his own brother, Ferdinand Maximilian Joseph, who had managed to get himself proclaimed Emperor of Mexico in 1864 and then, having been captured by Mexican revolutionaries, was executed by a firing squad in Mexico in 1867. Second heir was Crown Prince Rudolf, Franz Joseph's son, who famously died inexplicably at Mayerling in 1889. Next in line was the Archduke Karl Rudolf, the Emperor's younger brother. In the spring of 1896 he went on a pilgrimage to the Holy Land where, determined to play the part of his devotions to the hilt, he insisted on drinking from the River Jordan - despite being warned that the water was alive with disease - and promptly died of typhoid fever in May. By 1898 Karl Rudolf's son was the improbable heir to the throne: the 35-year-old Archduke Franz Ferdinand.

It must be said that Franz Ferdinand was not a very popular individual, even among Austrians. He was an enthusiastic supporter of Dr Karl Leuger, the mayor of Vienna and leader of the antisemitic Christian Socialist Party (and a major influence on the opinions and creed of one Adolf Hitler). But Franz Ferdinand also hated the Hungarians, a somewhat bizarre prejudice as they made up a large part of his empire. In return, he was not liked by his peoples, nor, for that matter, by the Emperor himself, who had disapproved of his morganatic marriage to Sofie and ensured that his children should not inherit the Imperial throne. In fact, just about the only personal friend that Franz Ferdinand had among the Courts of Europe was Wilhelm II, who would be a welcome guest at the archduke's palace, which was best noted for the gruesome testimony to his one passion in life, hunting, in the shape of thousands of trophies to his prowess with the 'sporting' gun.

The programme of events for that Sunday, the 28th June, held no promise of excitement for the royal party. Upon arrival at Sarajevo, they would inspect a small body of troops before driving to the city hall for a formal welcome speech from the mayor and lunch, to be followed by another military inspection and then a tour of a carpet factory, before returning to the station for their overnight journey back to Vienna. A small party of conspirators was waiting for them.

Gavrilo Princip was a young Serbian student from a poor background, who had not helped himself by being a poor achiever. What he excelled in was a hatred for the Austro-Hungarian suppressor, which he saw as the enemy of the Greater Serbia in which he believed. His views were shared with young Nedeljko Cabrinovic, who also came from a poor background and also was a poor achiever.

There was no specific reason why they chose Franz Ferdinand as their target for assassination - he merely symbolised Austria-Hungary, the oppressor of Serb nationalism, and was handy on the spot here in Sarajevo. They had been trained by a shadowy Serbian terrorist group which was managed in very high places, not just in the military but also in the Serb government - and maybe beyond, for nothing was done in the Belgrade government that was not directed by Russia. Certainly, that was the view in Berlin, and London. They were probably right.

Having been supplied information about the archduke's programme, and facilitated passage into Bosnia by Serbian government officials, five conspirators got ready in Sarajevo, but three lost their nerve, leaving the job to be done by Princip, who had a pistol and a bomb in his pocket, and Cabrinovic, armed with a bomb (they could not afford any more hand guns).

The Imperial motorcade was travelling slowly along the Appel Quay in bright sunshine, when Cabrinovic threw his bomb. The archduke's driver saw it coming and speeded up, so that it bounced off the folded-down roof, and exploded without harm to the archduke, injuring one of his entourage behind. The archduke, himself, was not in the least surprised when the bomb was thrown, and calmly ordered the visit to carry on, so they proceeded to the city hall, where the mayor made a rather ridiculous speech about the loyalty of the Bosnian people and their joy at his visit. The archduke interrupted him with justifiable annoyance, but the mayor, extremely unnerved by the outburst and not a little confused (he had not been told of the journey's events), resumed his speech.

Leaving the city hall, the archduke demanded to go to the hospital where his injured aide had been taken, and so they had to make a new itinerary. There followed some confusion on the way, because his driver had not been told of the change of plan, and turned right off Appel Quay, following the original route, and so the car and had to stop and reverse. By a twist of fate, another terrorist was standing there, ready to seize the chance of immortality.

Princip was hemmed in by the press of spectators, so was unable to reach into his pocket for his bomb, and so produced his gun. His Serb trainers never had been able to improve his poor marksmanship, indeed his fellow conspirators had derided his bad aim during target practice; but that was not a problem now, for the archduke was in point blank range. So Princip stepped forward with his revolver. What followed was witnessed by the archduke's aide, Count Franz von Harrach:

As the car quickly reversed, a thin stream of blood spurted from His Highness's mouth onto my right check. As I was pulling out my handkerchief to wipe the blood away from his mouth, the Duchess cried out to him, "For God's sake! What has happened to you?" At that she slid off the seat and lay on the floor of the car, with her face between his knees. I had no idea that she too was hit and thought she had simply fainted with fright. Then I heard His Imperial Highness say, "Sophie, don't die. Stay alive for the children!"

At that, I seized the Archduke by the collar of his uniform, to stop his head dropping forward and asked him if he was in great pain. He answered me quite distinctly, "It is nothing!"

His face began to twist somewhat but he went on repeating, six or seven times, ever more faintly as he gradually lost consciousness, "It's nothing!"

Then came a brief pause followed by a convulsive rattle in his throat, caused by a loss of blood. This ceased on arrival at the governor's residence.

The two unconscious bodies were carried into the building where their deaths were soon established. The news was met in Vienna with neither rejoicing nor much mourning. People really did not care all that much. The Emperor ordered a very low-key funeral, without even inviting foreign representatives and, when the Kaiser showed up any way, to mourn for his good friend, he was humiliatingly turned away. What the Austro-Hungarian government feared out of the assassination, was getting de-stabilised in the Balkans, and it had no intention of letting itself get de-stabilised. It quite rightly saw the smoking gun of the whole plot in the hand of Belgrade and seized the opportunity to crush Serbian nationalism right now, without delay, before catastrophe followed in the form of a Greater Serbia dominating the region.

Consequently, on the 13th July, Austria-Hungary delivered an ultimatum to the Serbian government which amounted to a humiliation[14], demanding that the Serbian government pledge *to suppress every publication which shall incite to hatred and contempt of the Monarchy, and the general tendency of which shall be directed against the territorial integrity of the latter... to eliminate without delay from public instruction in Serbia, everything, whether connected with the teaching corps or with the methods of teaching, that serves or may serve to nourish the propaganda against Austria-Hungary ... to agree to the cooperation in Serbia of the organs of the Imperial and Royal Government in the suppression of the subversive movement directed against the integrity of the Monarchy... to institute a judicial inquiry against every participant in the conspiracy of the twenty-eighth of June who may be found in Serbian territory; the organs of the Imperial and Royal Government delegated for this purpose will take part in the proceedings held for this purpose...*

---

[14] The Original can be accessed via www.lib.byu.edu/index.php/The_Austro-Hungarian_Ultimatum_to_Serbia

Incredibly, far from impudently refusing such insulting terms, the Serbian government replied before the demanded deadline, accepting all the terms except for two. This did not serve Vienna's purpose at all, though; the demands were a mere formality to its real priority, of seizing the troublesome country, and on the 28th July declared war on Serbia.

If it can be put down to one, single act, it was not that of Germany, or Russia, or Gavrilo Princip, which committed the world to war, but Austria-Hungary's mobilization against Serbia. Rivalry between Russia and Austria for control in the Balkans had been steadily intensifying when, in 1879, Vienna signed an alliance with Berlin to ensure that neither Germany nor Austria would find itself isolated in a war with Russia. At the same time, though, Bismarck did not want to alienate the Russian Bear and risk an alliance between St Petersburg and Paris, for the endless resources of the 'Sleeping Giant' would put Germany in peril once the old enmity with France broke out again, as it surely would, one day. As a result, Bismarck forged close contact with the Tsar and they signed the secret Reinsurance Treaty in 1887, whose tone towards the Habsburgs verged on the hostile.

In 1890, though, the Kaiser foolishly ignored Bismarck's tenets and declined to renew the Reinsurance Treaty. The consequence was not slow in coming, when France and Russia formed an alliance, odd as it was, between the most absolute of monarchies and the mother of republics. But it was a great success, leading to massive investment by France in Russian industry, and close social ties between the two countries which out-lived the Russian Revolution. More fatefully still, within two years France and Russia had a military agreement which bound them in mutual support should either country become engaged in a war in Europe.

Now, in July 1914, that war was at hand. Russia, patron of Slav brotherhood, would not stand by and see her old enemy Austria repress Serbia, and a few hours later Russia ordered partial mobilization, limited to those areas that would be relevant to war with Austria-Hungary. Just one look at the map of 1914 shows how Silesia stood between Austria-Hungary and Russia. Whether or not Germany wanted a war, it could not allow the protagonists to march through the estates of Silesia, and so, even though it felt shackled to the corpse of the crumbling dynasty of Austria-Hungary through the Triple Alliance, it had nothing better in place, so boldly announced its support for Vienna. How could it have done otherwise? To the people of Silesia and in the drawing rooms of Imperial Berlin, it made sound sense, and if war with Russia and France had to follow, then they had no choice. They were right of course; so, Russia now had to order full mobilization in order to face up to the might of Germany as well.

Every German understood the risks, but they could not permit Austria-Hungary to be defeated. The third member of the Triple Alliance, Italy, was deeply hostile to such a course, though. On the 31st July, the German Ambassador at Rome, Baron Ludwig von Flotow, had a meeting with Italy's Minister Marquis San Giuliano, in which Rome's perspective was made very clear indeed. The Marquis, in Flotow's words, *was in a state of great excitement*, since Italy had not been informed in advance of Austria's action against Serbia, and could with less reason be expected to take part in the war, as Italian interests were being directly injured by the Austrian action. The interview was a stormy one, in which Giuliano emphasised the grievances which his country had against Austria-Hungary, which, as he said, continued…

so persistently with a recognized injury to Italian interests, as to violate Article 7 of the Triple Alliance treaty, and because she was declining to give a guarantee for the independence and integrity of Serbia. He regretted that the Imperial Government had not done more to intervene in this connection to persuade Austria to a timely compliance.

It was very clear, that if Berlin did not support Rome against Vienna, then Rome would not support Berlin in its impending European crisis. Flotow duly reported the Marquis's dread assurance:

that the Italian Government had considered the question thoroughly, and had again come to the conclusion that Austria's procedure against Serbia must be regarded as an act of aggression, and that consequently a casus foederis, according to the terms of the Triple Alliance treaty, did not exist. Therefore Italy would have to declare herself neutral.

Flotow did not give up all hope of a change in Italy's position but shrewdly summed up Rome's outlook with the comment:

it cannot be denied that the attitude England has assumed has decidedly diminished prospects of Italian participation in our favour.

France now was bound to stand by Russia, through her treaty obligations - just as Germany knew. But let us pause for a moment, and ask, just how culpable was Germany in all this? The powerful and influential voices of Silesia were calling for protection, but in the wider scheme of Germany's ambitions for a Place in the Sun, there was no question of any gain for Germany, for there was no hope that the country's new Imperialism could benefit with a single new possession out of such a war. In truth, Germany saw herself in a defensive position here, having watched with increasing alarm the growing strength of Russia, thanks to French support. The longer that war was delayed, the more time Russia would have to grow even stronger. Already, Germany's encirclement had been completed; was Germany's strategy to bring Russia into conflict while it still had a chance to beat her?

In fact, German foreign policy, in the hands of Foreign Secretary Jagow and Chancellor Bethman Hollweg, was much more intelligent than that. They really were gambling on peace, with a strategy to force Russia on the Serbian question, to feel the burden of responsibility and decide whether she wanted to be the one to bring a war down around the ears of Europe. Maybe, if put in this light, Russia might fear that her allies - France and, probably, Britain - would shrink from supporting her if they feared that the belligerent in all this was Russia. It might be enough for Russia to pull back from the brink. The downstream consequence could achieve even more advantage for Germany, with a sporting chance of breaking the allies' encirclement of Germany, and then to create a new pattern of European alliances, maybe even a Russo-German alliance, which inevitably would benefit Berlin far more than the current treaty shackling it to the Austro-Hungarian corpse. Moreover, if the burden were placed on Russia, and she mobilized, she would convey to the world the message that she, not Germany, wanted war at any price. Jagow and Bethman Hollweg reckoned that they could then isolate the Austrian-Serb conflict and turn it to their advantage.

So, paradoxically, Germany's actions in these fateful, last few days before war, had nothing to do with Imperial expansion, but with defence. There was only one essential feature, but it was pivotal to the tight-rope walk between success and failure of their strategy: at all costs they had to keep political control over the crisis. Clausewitz summed it up:

The leading lines of war have always been determined by cabinets, a practice which is fully in accord with 'the nature of things' since none of the principal plans for war can be separated from political considerations[15].

---

[15] Clausewitz, C, 1832, On War, unfinished but published posthumously by his widow

Truth to tell, this betrayed the fatal weakness of the German cabinet, because, in shifting the burden of responsibility for the next decision, Berlin necessarily relinquished control over the situation, and left the shots to be called by Austria-Hungary and Russia.

So, the risk was taken, and lost. Russia was mobilizing, and only one result could follow: Schlieffen's plan had to be put into action at once. The awful fact is that, at the eleventh hour, the Kaiser wanted to pull back from the brink himself; but it was too late. He formally wrote to St Petersburg insisting upon a cessation of Russia's mobilization and its challenge to the Triple Alliance. Russia refused; and on Saturday, the 1st August the Kaiser signed the Declaration: *His Majesty the Emperor, my august Sovereign, in the name of the German Empire, accepts the challenge, and considers himself at war with Russia.*

At 17.00 that afternoon, the Regimental Headquarters of the 3rd Uhlans at Fürstenwalde received the short telegram[16]:

Mobilization. First day of mobilization 2nd August.

To all of European manhood, the world seemed to be embarking on a stern but glorious path to Maintain the Right, as each country saw it. Indeed, Otto had dived enthusiastically into the *Kultur* of his people and now expressed enthusiasm to put his own life at the disposal of his Fatherland. But in the quiet halls of his innermost thoughts, what was he really thinking? He was not born to the career of a soldier and did not pretend otherwise: he was a lawyer, with an excellent grasp of his profession and a distinguished career to look forward to. Indeed, at a time when Germans of his class always posed for photographs in the

---

[16] Regimental history and diaries, passim, Zipfel, E, 1931, Geschitchte des Ulanengeiments 'Kaiser Alexander II von Russland' (1 Brandenburgischen) nr 3, Zeulenroda, Thuringen

uniform of their unit, of which they were so proud, the only photograph which we have of Otto, has him in a smart, professional civilian suit, self-assertive, almost out-staring the viewer, definitely every inch a lawyer. Perhaps that side of his personality outshone the military side; if so, it would have been seen by some of his class - and of his Regiment - as a serious weakness. After all, their patron saint, Carl von Clausewitz, was scathingly dismissive of lawyers, and here was Otto, already well-qualified and appointed to the Higher Civil Service, to sit as a junior judge.

All that we have, is a letter, which he wrote to his father, but it tells us much about this deep, intelligent young man, and his own family:

Friedeberg, 1 August, 1914

My Dear Papa

Mobilization has just begun, the prospect of peace has passed away. Tomorrow at 2.00 am I shall be at Regimental Headquarters at Furstenwalde.

I would like to send you heartfelt greetings. This is a heavy hour for everybody, but we look to the future courageously and with confidence. God will stand by us. Dear Papa, what heavy trials you have endured, particularly our dear mother's illness, which must have caused you such sorrow. But now you must be proud: you send your sons to the defence of the Fatherland in this time of war. You served honourably in the war 1870/71 and we want to emulate you. Robert's profession is soldiering. We know that he is determined to prove his soldierly virtues. But I also draw courage in this war. I pray to God, that He gives me bravery and skill, with which I will honourably fight and will bear the fearful challenge well, and that Robert and I will be assured of His gracious protection.

We all hope that we will see each other again in this world, after the war is over, but we do not know that. Because of that I would like to say to you, that you are the dearest thing on earth to me, and I express my sincere love and my thanks. I have often thought, that you were all goodness to me and how you have helped me through life. Up until now I have hardly expressed my gratitude, but I hope that you forgive me. I know I have often given into weakness, been dissatisfied with myself, been selfish and depressed, but these states of mind pass away, and I am pleased with all the goodness and beauty that I have in the world. For all that I send you my deepest, heartfelt thanks, my dear, good father. May all of us not be parted for long.

To my dearest Aunt Mariechen I send my heartfelt thanks. I will never forget, what you have done for us and what that means to us.

My sister Amelie I also give my heartfelt greetings. I pray to God, that your adorable, sunny and joyful disposition will not be far away.

My thoughts are with you daily, and I know that your thoughts are with us.

The call now -

With God for King and Fatherland!

Your loving Otto

PS Could I please leave you to settle my affairs.

Hidden deep inside this letter, are some clues which nobody could have foreseen would have had such an impression upon Otto's fate, and it is only with the benefit of hindsight, gained from the analysis of some old records that somehow survived a hundred years of upheaval, that they lead us to some profound conclusions. Otto refers to the heavy trials which his father had to endure; this was perplexing on first reading because, at that time, evidence had not come to light of the mental condition inherited from his mother; this only became clear from references in surviving medical records from Otto's captivity. His mother's condition must have cast a dark shadow over the family, but we have no evidence as to how she was treated. Clearly their Aunt Mariechen was a huge comfort: perhaps a housekeeper, surrogate mother and friend of the children, at a time when they needed a mother most.

Whether the family knew that the condition was hereditary is not known, but Otto clearly admitted his own psychological unhappiness – perhaps unconnected by his family with their mother's illness – which would later trouble the British military doctors who watched his condition deteriorate. Right now, though, Otto brushed aside his depression, and steeled himself for war.

WAR[17]

The 3rd Uhlans advance.

You don't have a cushy life in the cavalry!

How often had the youngsters heard the old soldiers singing that in some old marching song, as they rode back to Fürstenwalde from field training in the Rauener Mountains and in the magnificent forests around them, which the 3rd Uhlans loved so well in the halcyon days of peace. But, unbeknown to them, those days of perfect memory were growing more distant and irretrievable with every kilometre post which the trains passed as they rattled westwards at the regulation rate.

---

[17] Grateful thanks *passim* to the Public Records Office (Now the National Archive): Of the thousands of documents held, few have a reference with any probative value to the fate of Otto Scholz, but a large number provided primary resource material. See, for example: FO383/287; 383/420; WO 95; WO 157; WO 161; WO 900/45

While one Squadron was to remain at Fürstenwalde as a depôt Squadron, the rest would proceed to the Front under their commanding officer, *Oberstleutnant* von Linsingen, a true Prussian aristocrat of the old school if ever there was one. The regular officers were all noblemen, with Counts such as *Rittmeister* Graf von Wartensleben, Princes like *Leutnant* Stephan Alexander Viktor Prinz zu Schaumburg-Lippe, and of course, the 'vons' of the landed gentry who dominated the crème of society, including the Regimental Adjutant, *Leutnant* von Prittwitz und Gaffron, the son of a German dynasty that had been powerful in Silesia since the Middle Ages. Count von Götzen had famously taken Georg von Prittwitz und Gaffron with him on his adventures in Africa, while the 66-year-old General Maximilian von Prittwitz und Gaffron was now in command of the entire defence of Otto's homeland from attack by Russia. So proud to be counted still as a 3rd Uhlan was General of Cavalry von Kleist, an extremely highly-decorated officer, with the coveted *Pour Le Mérite*, the Kingdom of Prussia's highest military order, perhaps more famously known since 1916 as the 'Blue Max'. Three subalterns from the von Kleist family were also serving in the Regiment; Heinrich was an *Oberleutnant* in the Reserve, commissioned in 1910 but he was killed in 1915, after the Regiment had moved to the bleak Eastern Front, facing the Russian host. The two others were youngsters who would serve in the latter part of the war, when the Regiment was in the trenches of the Western Front; but Ewald was killed on the 18th September 1918, while Fedor lingered on until he, too, died, on the 3rd February, 1919[18].

The 3rd Uhlans were going to fight alongside the 2nd Dragoons, another Brandenburg Regiment, with a history dating back to 1689, making it

---

[18] Rangliste der Königlich Preussischen Armee für 1913, Ernst Siegfried Mittler und Sohn, Berlin

the oldest Regiment of dragoons in the German Army. Their history had earned them the distinction of velvet black facings and a miniature Prussian eagle on their caps. The eagle badge was a unique tradition which was awarded to them after an action in the 1812 war against France, when a detail of 2nd Dragoons were riding their horses bareback to water, when they were ambushed by some French cavalry, but still managed to beat off their attackers. They were based in Schwedt, on the Oder River, and commanded by *Oberst* Maximilian von Poseck, a highly-respected officer who would survive the war and write the definitive work on the fortunes of the German cavalry in those early days of the war in Belgium and France[19]. Together, these two Regiments displayed all that was finest in the Prussian military machine, forming the 5th Cavalry Brigade, under the command of Colonel von Arnim, from an old Silesian family which famously had commanded the 2nd Uhlans in 1867, and which made it something of a family matter, for the 3rd Uhlans' brigade ordnance officer was *Leutnant* von Arnim, like Otto, in the Officer Reserve.

The 5th Cavalry Brigade was to serve in the 2nd Cavalry Corps. The Army's cavalry was organised into four corps, of which the 2nd Cavalry Corps was on the right wing, the vanguard of the whole 2nd Army, under the command of *Generalleutnant* von der Marwitz. The Marwitz family was another noble Silesian dynasty; *Leutnant* von der Marwitz was a troop leader in the 1st Squadron of the 3rd Uhlans, while young Ensign Gebhard von der Marwitz joined the Regiment in time for the war (only to be killed on the 1st December).

It was the 2nd Cavalry Corps' mission to ensure that the advance of the whole Front Line, between Antwerp, Brussels and Charleroi, succeeded

---

[19] Poseck, M von, 1923, The German Cavalry 1914 in Belgium and France, republished 2007 Naval and Military Press, Uckfield E Sussex

against the resistance of the Belgian Army, and possibly against a landing by British troops. Then, they knew, they would be facing French troops that by then would be in Northern Belgium, so they would be feeling out the enemy, gaining information, maybe locked in bitter fights, surely hitting them in shock actions, to win through and advance westwards, in General Schlieffen's grand plan to encircle Paris and hit the French Army in the rear. They learned very quickly the value of the wagon-mounted machine gun units on the regimental strength, while the Brigade was supported by the light, mobile guns of the 35th Field Artillery Regiment, to give some shelling support when it was most needed.

Alongside the 5th Cavalry Brigade, there were two other brigades in the 2nd Corps. The 8th Cavalry Brigade, consisted of the 7th Kurassiers (heavy cavalry resplendent on parade in lobster-tailed helmets and body-armour) and the 12th Hussars. It was, however, the Life-Hussar Brigade which were the social and military élite of the Corps; certainly, that is what they would have told you. The 1st and 2nd Life Hussars, which constituted the Brigade, were under the command of *Oberst* von Frankenberg und Ludwigsdorf. Hussars originated in the wild, light horsemen of Hungary, and the Life Hussars guarded their cachet jealously; they swept many a young girl off her feet, but that should not convey the impression that they merely strutted around looking the part; they had good reason to wear the Death's Head badge with pride.

Amid the August heatwave, the business of mobilization was carried out according to a minutely-detailed, pre-arranged timetable. The 3rd Uhlans were especially proud that they were to be one of the first Regiments to engage the enemy and, from the Colonel to the raw recruit, every man did his utmost to achieve mobilization without a hitch. So polished was the process, that they were able to finish the job and then have a full hour in the Regiment's shrine, the Garrison church of St Marien, to celebrate Holy Communion - for many, it would be for the last time.

The next day, the 2nd August, the 1st Squadron and the Regimental Staff were ready to leave their garrison home at Fürstenwalde, escorted to the station by the cheering inhabitants. The other Squadrons followed during the night. Men and horses embarked on an exhausting railway journey towards Belgium, following von Moltke's orders, in turn carrying out - although, fatally, modifying - a plan formulated in 1892 by General Schlieffen for a strategic victory in Europe. It seemed the essence of simplicity, but not a thing had been overlooked.

The whole process had been planned according to the most detailed railway timetable that demanded absolute punctuality with the troop trains and even regulated their speed. The journey to their allotted deployment zone was to run at 30 kilometres per hour. Enough time, on board, then, for them to gather their thoughts about the coming days. Every hope was pinned on it being a fine cavalry action. As they travelled through the German fatherland to the border, they had complete trust in the justice of the German cause. The jubilation of the inhabitants was fantastic. At every place through which they passed, they were cheered and feted. As the Regimental history put it,

That was the Spirit of 1914.

As the fine old soldiers' songs mingled with the monotonous rhythm of the wheels on the track, enthusiasm conquered all weariness and tension. The smooth mobilization gave everyone a great cause to feel success.

With the outbreak of war, the whole spectrum of the German People, from the aristocratic élite to the Socialists, abandoned their differences, their ideologies, and joined together instantaneously into one People, a single organism with seventy million heads yet possessing one soul, one will and one concept. This was the core of Germany's political identity, that owed everything to the lofty ideals of Prussian history, shaped by the autocracy that kept the Kaiser as their spiritual and temporal leader, and keeping democracy well under heel. It was a recipe for the Renaissance of Teutonic Feudalism, a Revival of the Age of Goethe. And yet, they were not looking back. Rather, they were looking forward, to a new European Revolution, a New Order which despised and rejected the petty Gallic cries of liberty, fraternity and equality. They looked down, also, on the British as a nation obsessed with the business of sea power and commerce, whose Army did not look upon soldiering as a profession so much as a sporting way of life.

In the new German nation, the highest human virtue - war - was their Torch of Life. As they interpreted the true ethic of Darwinism, war delivered the supreme state. The victor in war was the rightful ruler of man, and Germany worshipped at the feet of its war heroes, from the Teutonic knights of the Middle Ages, to the Uhlans of 1914. This burned in the German soul, from hearth and home to the field of battle, with the dangerous fire of the zealot, determined to conduct the war with pride, with heads held high, certain in the knowledge that they are the chosen People of God.

The German High Command had been planning this for years. Count Alfred von Schlieffen, Chief of the German General Staff from 1891 to 1906, developed his master plan with an attack by seven massive armies, which depended on the strength being in the north - the right wing of the German offensive. France and Russia were deeply committed to each other, so that, if Germany were to go to war with one, it would rapidly find itself at war with the other. Schlieffen's plan, therefore, was to seize Paris as rapidly as possible, while the Russian giant was still mobilizing, and, once France had fallen, all the German war effort could be turned to defeating Mother Russia. There was just one problem: Belgium.

The French had built massive defences on the eastern border of their country with Germany, which, no doubt, looked quite awesome, and would undoubtedly give the Germans a hard time. But the German right wing planned to punch its way far to the north of those defences, through Belgium, and then swing down and encircle Paris, before pressing on and delivering a fatal blow in the rear of the French defenders in their mighty fortresses, reminiscent of the ancient Battle of Cannae. By invading Belgium, though, Germany knew that it risked bringing in Great Britain as an enemy. The British Army was not a problem – *We'll send the Berlin police to arrest it!* was the standing joke - but the Royal Navy was the Kaiser's real fear.

Whistling somewhat in the dark, in 1914 the Kaiser declared that *Germany's future is on the water* and, while Britain would wring her hands over honouring her commitment to rescue Belgium from invasion, she was in no doubt that a victorious Germany in Europe would gain control of the Continental Channel ports. From there it could destroy the lifeblood of the British Empire and the North Atlantic, her Merchant Fleet - from the Cunarders racing on the New York run to the rusty old steamers that, in the immortal poetry of Cicely Fox Smith, had *sampled all the harbour mud from Cardiff to Canton*. No, that could never happen - and the Royal Navy would be the Fleet's Protector. As former First Sea Lord Sir John Fisher observed, *the whole principle of naval fighting is to be free to go anywhere with every damned thing the Navy possesses*. The importance of keeping this principle in mind when contemplating a victorious Germany in Europe could not be underestimated.

In stark contrast to Germany's bold, meticulous plan of attack, the rationale of France's military defence was blind to reality. Just as the French Establishment was horrified that anybody should suggest that their soldiers should abandon the red trousers of tradition, the symbol of France's pride, the country's philosophy was dominated by one ambition, to recover Alsace Lorraine; and in the process, they ignored all reason. Indeed, 'Papa' Joffre's insistence that modern technology was irrelevant (his word) and that aircraft should be shunned, was bolstered by his unwavering belief that France would be successful in any military campaign simply by taking the offensive, by striking hard with the sword and the bayonet in neo-Napoleonic fashion. This, he insisted, would inevitably win the day. He was at the very top, there was nobody to contradict him; anybody who dared to contradict or disappoint him was doomed to be shunted into the sidings of history.

The French loved it; indeed, amidst the gaiety of France's *Belle Epoch* it complemented perfectly the culture of French life, a culture over which the Kaiser himself drooled with envy and, yet, which remained unattainable for him. Theirs was a culture which breathed a style that nobody could match - and it was as evident in the Army as in the streets of Paris. At the very top were the heavy cavalry Regiments known as the Cuirassiers; they had been there for a hundred years, and meant to keep it that way. Napoleon created heroes out of them, and they returned the favour with glory at his greatest battles; indeed, to the British they were 'Bonaparte's Bodyguard'. Perhaps it was inevitable that they would only accept the very best, in all its forms and styles.

The late American military historian, Colonel John Elting, offers quite possibly an apocryphal tale that one French Cuirassier Regiment created the ultimate test to establish whether an aspiring officer was suitable to join them: he was given three horses, three bottles of champagne and three women; and he would have three hours in which to finish the champagne, seduce all three women and ride a 20-mile course[20]. Their Napoleonic heritage proved so enduring that, in August 1914, they went to war wearing the same head-dress and body armour in which they had covered themselves with glory from Austerlitz to Waterloo. The artist whose work found itself in Otto's Regimental records even portrayed them thus, as the Uhlans cut them down.

France's answer to the anticipated German advance, Plan 17, paid scant heed to the risks of German invasion by striking through Belgium and then swinging down south to take Paris before storming the central French defences in the rear. Instead, Plan 17 had been devised by General Joffre, who had been appointed Minister of War and Chief of the General Staff in 1911, based on the strategy of the offensive *à Outrance* - a massive attack by French troops through the German centre. In that way they would recover France's pride lost in the Franco-Prussian war and take back Alsace Lorraine, the armoured Cuirassiers closely supported by the conspicuously red-trousered infantry, marching victoriously to Berlin. Even when it dawned upon them, that the weight of the German force was in the north, they stupidly thought, so much the better, for the German centre would necessarily be weaker, allowing them to punch their way through to victory.

With the mechanism of that precision instrument which was the German war machine, on the 2nd August the Germans formally requested that Belgium permit them free passage to French soil:

Reliable information has been received by the German Government to the effect that French forces intend to march on the line of the Meuse by Givet and Namur. This information leaves no doubt as to the intention of France to march through Belgian territory against Germany.

---

[20] Elting, J, 1997, Sword Around A Throne, Perseus Books

The German Government cannot but fear that Belgium, in spite of the utmost goodwill, will be unable, without assistance, to repel so considerable a French invasion with sufficient prospect of success to afford an adequate guarantee against danger to Germany. It is essential for the self-defence of Germany that she should anticipate any such hostile attack. The German Government would, however, feel the deepest regret if Belgium regarded as an act of hostility against herself the fact that the measures of Germany's opponents force Germany, for her own protection, to enter Belgian territory.

This was bullying on a breath-taking scale, and only marginally tempered by promises to evacuate Belgium and restore its independence, once Germany had won the war. If Belgium co-operated with a friendly attitude, Germany would pay in cash for all the necessaries for her troops as they passed through, and to pay an indemnity for any damage that may have been caused by German troops. But if Belgium resisted the German advance, *Germany will, to her regret, be compelled to consider Belgium as an enemy.* It was a dark threat of destruction to force the Belgians to comply.

But Belgium did not falter. The next morning, the Belgian Minister for Foreign Affairs delivered a note to the German Minister in Brussels:

This note has made a deep and painful impression upon the Belgian Government.... The treaties of 1839, confirmed by the treaties of 1870 vouch for the independence and neutrality of Belgium under the guarantee of the Powers, and notably of the Government of His Majesty the King of Prussia.

With enormous dignity, the Belgian note emphasised that they had always been faithful to they international obligations, and expected their neighbours to do the same: *The attack upon her independence with which the German Government threaten her constitutes a flagrant violation of international law. No strategic interest justifies such a violation of law.*

The reply from Brussels left Berlin in no doubt that Belgian would fight back and defend itself against the violation of her neutrality. It was a brave assertion for a last stand against the might of the world's strongest Army. But, shrugged the German High Command, so be it. There was no turning back now, the great war machine was in gear, and moving forward.

The train journey to the border had been dreadful for the 3rd Uhlans, hot, slow and exhausting, both for men and horses. The relief of disembarking was indescribable, but there was no time to rest and recover. This was the assembly point for the 2nd Cavalry Division, and von Schlieffen's plan demanded that there was no time to pause. It was 09.30 on the 4th August, and Otto and his Regiment were standing mounted, right on the Belgian frontier at a place called Gemmenich, near the strategic point where the frontiers of Germany, Belgium and the Netherlands meet. The order was given to advance and an almighty *Hurrah!* was shouted as the 3rd Uhlans crossed the border into Belgium. Otto's war had begun.

Speed was essential to the German strategy and Otto's troopers had to spearhead the advance fast and efficiently. Moving all the time, concentrating on the job in hand, one wonders whether they would have given much thought to the ultimatum that Britain indeed served. They certainly would not have been surprised; in any case, everybody was elated that first day, as they swept into Belgium. There had been a high-risk factor of a British response, but a swift *pusch* to take Paris would bring the whole campaign to a close in six weeks. No doubt they would take the British in their stride. No doubt.

Paradoxically, the thread in the complex web which pulled Britain into the war had been spun in order to guarantee peace. The wars against Napoleon, which culminated in the Allied victory at Waterloo in 1815, had left all sorts of dreadful legacies for the British Government, from an impoverished Treasury that had been hard-pressed to pay for it, to social discontent with 300,000 redundant and unemployable soldiers and sailors roaming the streets. So, to avoid such a thing happening again, Britain needed to orchestrate some sort of diplomatic deal that would keep Continental Europe from breaking out in war again. On the face of it, the solution they found was masterly. It could have lasted a thousand years.

That corner of Northwest Europe known as Belgium had been a cockpit of fighting for centuries. For most of its history it had been part of the Netherlands, indeed it was in this guise that Belgians fought at Waterloo in 1815. In that universal struggle of mankind to win its right to govern its own destiny, the people of Belgium rose up against the Netherlands in 1830. Very quickly the governing powers of Europe appreciated that Belgium had won its State Rights, and Austria, Britain, France, Prussia and Russia met in London to forge a new Treaty that would guarantee Belgian independence and, at the same time, eliminate the risks of another European war such as Napoleon's, which had left Europe in ruins. Of course, the Dutch strongly opposed the loss of its territory but, ultimately, it had to conceded defeat and the Treaty of London was finally concluded in 1839. In fact, although it became a sovereign State with its own monarch and legislative authority, it was never supremely comfortable in these new clothes, for it knew that the Allied powers had really conjured up its existence as a buffer state between the old antagonists in Europe, while Britain's undertaking to guarantee its neutrality merely enforced that notion.

With the benefit of hindsight, though, we are unsettled by that nagging little voice whispering into our ear, that the supervision of Belgian territorial rights could hardly be deemed a just cause for plunging the mighty British Empire into a European war. Indeed, greater threats had loomed in recent years, such as the Moroccan crisis, and war had been averted then. Most certainly, the Belgian government made it abundantly clear that they did not want any foreign power at all tramping over their land. Of course nobody, certainly not the Germans, expected permission to be granted for their armies to cross Belgian soil and when none was received the military machine just had to steamroller on, doubtless expecting an ultimatum from Britain at any time.

Whether the Germans guessed it or not, that ultimatum was not a foregone conclusion. The British Cabinet was awkwardly split over the wisdom of intervention, and a looming financial catastrophe argued persuasively against mobilising in the Continental war. The trouble was, that the key decision-makers such as the Foreign Secretary, Sir Edward Grey, and Winston Churchill, were champing at the bit to support France irrespective of any diplomatic alliances - a sentiment that was not shared by much of the British population, who cared little for the *entente cordiale* with Paris and rather liked the German barbers and waiters who had settled in their home towns. It was a nerve-snapping time in the Cabinet office, and threats of resignations had to be contended with while steering a course which, however hazardous, inevitably confronted mobilisation against Germany. Meanwhile, Lord Grey was walking a very slippery diplomatic tightrope, making promises to the French of British backing which, at the time they were made, were simply not true.

As the country sweltered in the August Bank Holiday weekend of 1914, the British Cabinet was awkwardly split over the wisdom of intervention in the Continental war that was now breaking out with Imperial Germany poised to march through Belgium and attack France – but the fateful decision had to be made. On the 3rd August, Britain's Foreign Secretary, Sir Edward Grey, rose to his feet in the House of

Commons, and the speech which followed changed the face of Great Britain for ever:

We have got the consideration of Belgium which prevents us [also] from any unconditional neutrality, and, without those conditions absolutely satisfied and satisfactory, we are bound not to shrink from proceeding to the use of all the forces in our power. If we did take that line by saying, ""We will have nothing whatever to do with this matter" under no conditions—the Belgian Treaty obligations, the possible position in the Mediterranean, with damage to British interests, and what may happen to France from our failure to support France—if we were to say that all those things mattered nothing, were as nothing, and to say we would stand aside, we should, I believe, sacrifice our respect and good name and reputation before the world, and should not escape the most serious and grave economic consequences[21].

There is no evidence that there was actually a division on the ultimatum to Germany – it was a speech, not a motion, so no vote was taken. As the final hours ticked away, late on the 3rd August, John Spender, editor of the Westminster Gazette, was with Sir Edward Grey in the Foreign Secretary's office, and they were standing at the window looking out into the sunset across St. James's Park, as the lamplighters were lighting the first street lamps along the Mall, when Sir Edward said,

The lamps are going out all over Europe, and we shall not see them lit again in our lifetime.

Great Britain's ultimatum to Germany expired at 23.00 on the 4th August 1914 (midnight Berlin time). The world was at war.

---

[21] The original Hansard transcript; see
www.hansard.millbanksystems.com/commons/1914/aug/03/statement-by-sir-edward-grey

The French had committed the vastness of its Army; but a modestly-sized British Expeditionary Force was all that the Cabinet could offer and, much to the disgust of France, a modestly-sized British Expeditionary Force was all they would get. 90,000 men sailed for France, to protect the northern flank of the French Army which numbered some 1,300,000 men, against seven German armies of regulars and reservists, estimated at something over 5 million men.

Sometimes, though, the numbers game makes fools of the players. It was right at the start of their advance, that the Uhlans got a real shock; time and time again, they found, they were not just dealing with the Belgian Army, but also with extreme, bitter resistance from the civilian population, people who would sell their lives dearly for every yard of ground. The Germans' surprise is expressed well in the 3rd Uhlans' Regimental history, which says that the Belgian government had planned a *franctireur* campaign, with cyclists taking word of the advance to the next town or village, where the people would shoot at German troops from copses and from houses, *even from church towers* in the words of the Regimental records.

In fact, the German soldiers' grandfathers had encountered *franctireurs* in the Franco-Prussian War, and they had been just as outraged then, as well. Far from harbouring barbarous intentions to civilians, the Teutonic Code strove to keep them well out of the business of war; indeed, the German High Command had laid down precise rules about the treatment of the civilian population. The people were not to be regarded as enemies and were free to continue their normal life. The High Command stressed that severe punishments would be ordered on any soldier who harmed, or robbed, or even insulted an enemy civilian: that was the German Code. Accordingly, it was expected that civilians would not, in any way, take up arms against them.

It was, therefore, with a feeling of disgust that the advancing Germans found themselves ambushed, fired on and terrorised by French civilians in 1870, when the word *franctireur* was coined, in what was their first experience of Total War. The noble Code of War demanded that warrior fight against warrior, there was no place in their Code for these irregulars who had no military calling and in peace-time were not even called upon to assemble. They were deadly effective at harassing the Germans then and now, in 1914, civilians were doing the very same thing. Particular outrage was expressed at how the *franctireurs* picked out single troopers and patrols. The 3rd Uhlans Regimental History stated:

Many a brave cavalryman was the victim of a bullet in an ambush. The fate of many a man never was discovered, he was simply shown as 'Missing'. You had to experience it, the bitter effect which this behaviour had on the troops; they only wanted to fight against the enemy Army - those were the Rules of Engagement which they understood.

This passage from the Regimental history of the 3rd Uhlans explain how the Germans felt so justified, now, to put an iron interpretation on Clausewitz's words: that *War knows of only one method: force.*

At 15.00 that afternoon, there was a skirmish at Visé, where the Regiment stood in reserve, ready to support the Germans in the firing line where they were most needed. The next day, the reconnaissance Squadron went forward, scouting ahead of the body of the division, which was to follow next day. It was dreary, rainy weather, when the 3rd Uhlans reached Navagne, and beyond, near Mouland, they had their baptism of fire, from the shells of the mighty forts defending Liege. In order to avoid unnecessary casualties, they withdrew and spent a further night in Fouron-le-Court, while reconnaissance patrols stealthily spied out the land ahead, to the wide, strong River Maas. The

1st Squadron was ordered to send a patrol out on the other side of the river, so the courageous *Leutnant* von der Marwitz left with a detail of 12 men. Only strong swimmers were picked. As they would be crossing under fire, they had to make it across very fast.

In the strong, storm-fed current, Corporal Bosdorf's horse drowned in the swirling waters; he only just made it to safety. On the opposite bank, the patrol split up into three groups (one corporal and two troopers), each party to reconnoitre their own designated area, observing where the enemy's positions were, and finding where the pioneers could best build their pontoon bridges and where the Division could ford the river. Von der Marwitz sent back reports that the crossings over the Liege Canal were free, but the bridges over the Maas had been blown. So, next day, the Regiment moved up to the Maas, ready to cross. It was raining torrentially, when von der Marwitz brought his patrol back, reporting that Uhlan Wohner was missing. No time could be lost, so all the available pontoon bridge wagons were brought up, while, in the meantime, the Pioneer Battalions got to work ferrying the cavalry across, three horses on each crossing, just where von der Marwitz had reported.

Long days in the saddle under the fierce heat of an August sun took a massive toll on the stamina of men and horses that had never had the chance to recover from that exhausting railway journey. They had been expecting to meet the challenging targets of the Schlieffen Plan; the Belgian resistance was slowing them down, they knew that, and if it had not been for the Pioneers, they would have been stranded, with no hope of advancing. Having crossed the river, they could press on, following behind the barrage of heavy artillery that was destroying everything in its path; but then they were reaching far beyond the point where the logistics of food and supply could catch up with them. A cavalry Regiment needs prodigious supplies of fodder and hard food for the horses, which was far bulkier than the human rations to bring forward. On the 8th August, von Linsingen wrote in the Regimental diary:

At 2.45 am the 2nd Cavalry Division set off for a bridgehead position. We came through devastated villages and towns and found them full of Franctireurs, in a shaken state. Heavy shells hit from Liège, several times in the square, causing countless casualties. Also heavy shell fire from siege artillery hit Liège. Standing in a field of oats, we fed the horses on the oats there. At 4 o'clock we advanced further to Bolre, where the 5th Cavalry Brigade was to be quartered, but it was very bad, dirty, insanitary; and here there were no oats to feed our horses.

They were advancing so fast, that lines of communication and stores were left far behind and there were no oats for the horses and no field kitchen for the men. They had to live off the land and stomach Belgian white bread and chocolate that they were able to 'liberate' from cafés and estaminets. On top of increasing fatigue, lack of proper food began to have an enervating effect; after all, Napoleon correctly observed that an Army marches on its stomach. Even at this early stage, it was clear that somebody had blundered in the grand plan: nobody, it seemed, had guessed that the all-important lines of communication that fed and armed the troops might not match the demands made of them, as they passed through enemy territory, on a timetable that demanded lightning advance.

Otto and his men were fighting for a famous victory, but were being let down by the faceless pen-pushers, safe at the rear. Still, they were Brandenburgers, they had been taught from infancy that they always had to do their duty. Today that sounds hackneyed, but in August 1914 it was the guiding light for the best blood in Europe. Even so, exhaustion and lack of proper food had a bad effect on morale, and their dreams of Paris alone could not fill their stomachs. But still they sang. It became the enduring recollection of the war for millions of Belgian and French witnesses in those early weeks. German soldiers sang their hearts out - every waking moment of the day. No doubt, for their morale; probably, in *Kameradschaft*; maybe, to stay awake in those desperate days of non-stop action. They never stopped singing. One of the most famous started:

Lieb Vaterland
Du hast nach bösen Stunden
Aus dunkler Tiefe einen neuen Weg gefunden
Ich liebe dich

Dear Fatherland
You have after bad hours
Found a new way out of dark depth
I love you

On the next day, the 9th August, they pressed on with the advance, now displaying more extreme caution in their reconnaissance as resistance became stronger. As they headed across Tongres to their objective at St Trond, they rode through street barricades, felled trees, trenches; anything that could be used had been thrown in their way, to slow them down while snipers shot at them from every vantage point that they could find. Tongres was a small town, once full of life, with a beautiful Gothic church. Now it was a makeshift fortress, doomed to fall. The description of the town's beauty in the Regimental history has a certain poignancy, almost regret; surprising sentiments for people whom history has branded as monsters. There was a job to be done, though, and the Uhlans had to carry out their duty.

The 2nd Squadron went ahead as reconnaissance Squadron, where the streets of Tongres were hotly defended; every barricade and house was a fortress. It could slow down progress of the advance badly and speed was becoming increasingly important as every day which passed saw resistance grow, endangering the strategy which depended on speed. To make matters worse, the chain of communication from the Front Line to the High Command had broken down badly. The Belgians had cut the telephone lines upon which so much depended in this tightly-planned advance, while telegrams often did not reach their destination for 24 hours - and still had to be decoded. The bridges, the roads and the railways had been blown, and even when the despatch riders were able to make some headway, they risked a sniper's bullet from every house and doorway.

The leader of the spearhead was a certain *Leutnant* Freiherr von Richthofen; he was made a lieutenant in the Regiment in June 1912, five months before his cousin Manfred was awarded his lieutenancy in the 1st Uhlans[22], another crack Prussian Regiment of lancers. Manfred, it was, who would later win immortality as the war's only hero, a flying ace known to the world as the Red Baron. Now *Leutnant* von Richthofen reached the position where the first of the fortified houses stood; without mincing his words he explained to the defenders the position - that is, their house would be razed to the ground if the barricade was not removed at once. In a few moments the street was clear and the Squadron triumphantly rode through the place, escorted by some carabineers on foot.

This was no time for niceties. The German High Command had underestimated Belgian resistance to invasion; after all, Germany had arrogantly but naively assured Belgium in advance, that it was merely using her sovereign country as a stepping-stone to attack France. It had

---

[22] Of the many biographies of von Richthofen, see Burrows, W, 1972, Richthofen, Mayflower, London

even been hoped that King Albert would simply order his Army to line the German route in silent protest. To Germany's dismay, the Belgians were putting up a massive resistance, threatening to slow down the crucial timetable for conquering France, and tying up troops in occupying Belgium which were sorely needed elsewhere. As much as the *franctireurs* were a shock to the German psyche, which lived on order and everything in its place (and civilians had no place in war), the German High Command had still anticipated this, hence the terror tactics which spawned a thousand stories in the world's press.

There is no doubt, that the Germans committed shocking atrocities in Belgium, killing innocent civilians, razing and looting whole towns, in an effort to instil terror into the hearts of the people, and make them cower. But, as the advance continued, the Belgians still defended every yard of ground. It was a vainglorious defence, and the people, and their King, Albert, were all but martyred by it; but at least they might delay the Germans long enough for help to arrive from across the Channel. For a little country, Belgium fought like a tiger; the gravestones in honour of the Belgian dead at Netley Hospital give bold testimony to that, as they were mortally wounded in the fighting and evacuated as fast as they could, finding themselves on British hospital trains which took them back to England, allies regardless of their uniform.

On the 10th August, at 05.00, *Leutnant* von Jagow, from the 1st Squadron of the 3rd Uhlans, left camp with a reconnaissance patrol to scout out the ground ahead. It was a punishing day's work, and they had been out for eleven hours when, at about 16.00, they reached the town of Orsmael-Gussenhoven, west of St Trond. The patrol had split up just before they got into town, as *Leutnant* von Jagow stayed on the edge of town to observe from some cover.

It was quiet here, they did not see anything of the enemy, and so they rode through the cobbled streets into the centre of town. It was there, that they were ambushed. A detail of Belgian lancers rushed out from a hostelry and opened fire on them, just as Belgian covering fire opened up along the whole of the main street in ambush. The whole patrol was caught in the open street, and soon was worn down to Corporal Striegan and two troopers. *Leutnant* von Jagow was wounded and taken prisoner, along with Ensign Freiherr von Czettriss and two troopers. Corporal Striegan had lost his horse, killed from under him, but then he saw a riderless horse, standing loose in a garden. With the help of his two comrades, he caught the horse and, together, they managed to get back to the Squadron. As darkness fell, they made for St Trond where they would bivouac for the night, but they would leave behind the bodies of two comrades from the reconnaissance patrol.

Meanwhile the 8th Cavalry Brigade and the Life-Hussar Brigade, which made up the rest of the Division, had its own problems at the crossroads at Orsmael-Gussenhoven, so the Uhlans would have to look after themselves. The 4th Squadron, Otto's Squadron, under the command of *Rittmeister* von Strantz, gave gunfire support to get the patrol out of trouble, in a brief skirmish with Belgian lancers who were supported by *franctireurs* (who wore a curious semblance of a uniform for fear of being dealt with as partisans, or spies, if caught).

A patrol of seven riders from the 4th Squadron, led by *Leutnant* von Kuhne, another Officer of the Reserve, had set out that morning to reconnoitre the area south-west of Herck, beyond St Trond to Tirlemont, to find out whether the place was in the hands of the enemy. When they got to 2 kilometres of Tirlemont, they left the high road, so that they could scout out the town unobserved. They were about 900 metres from the town when they saw some people, dressed in dark clothing, who had been concealed in a sunken lane, sloping down from the high road between St Trond and Tirlemont. Leaving the horses in the charge of a horse-holder, the patrol stealthily went on foot up to the high road. There, at the place where the sunken lane and the high road met, was a house. In front of the house were two male inhabitants, who had probably seen the Uhlans and gave away their position to others by giving signals. The patrol had no time to stop and deal with them, for they needed to get further and see what those darkly-clothed people were about. As they closed in, they could see that it was a company of enemy cyclists. It was then that a short burst of fire came from somewhere ahead of them, and suddenly they were under fire from three sides.

Their only escape route was back the way they came, but they were able to withdraw, and they got back to the horses. Then they rode on to Orsmael-Gussenhoven, as they had planned, not knowing what had befallen the others there. As they reached the town, they hit a hail of fire. Beside the high road, behind tall whitethorn hedges, were deep meadows, through which ran a wide water-channel. It actually ran through the town, the very direction that the Uhlans had to take. The Belgians had barricaded the high road in Orsmael-Gussenhoven but, luckily, had not bothered with the water-channel. By using the cover of the channel, leading their horses, they managed to get past the barricade, before the enemy spotted them, and all hell let loose.

As they battled their way through, every man was looking out for himself, and nobody noticed that *Leutnant* von Kuhne was getting further and further behind. Then Corporal Mitschke saw what had happened to von Kuhne. He was horrified to see that his poor horse was badly wounded, on the left side of his chest. With every step of the horse's courageous, noble, agonised gallop, blood gushed from the wound. Mitschke stopped and, despite the heavy fire that they were under, he went back to the horse, trying to calm him, and staunched the wound with a pack-bandage. On seeing him, his comrades stopped as well, even though they were under a hail of fire, but they needed to give him support as they saw the danger of the position he was in. When the bleeding from the wound had been staunched, it was possible to take that brave horse with them to St Trond, where he could be cared for. As they reached the last house in the town, though, the horse had become so weak through the trauma and the loss of blood, that he had to be put out of his misery. They had been in a lethal position in trying to save that horse, but they would not have hesitated to do the same thing again. Exhausted, they made it back to the Squadron that evening.

Time was pressing hard, as Otto's Regiment fought against ever more bitter resistance, and their confidence was rocked by the resistance which they had encountered from the Belgian civilians. The Germans paid homage to the art of war - it was a matter of contest between men of arms, according to their Prussian Code, and they were shocked to be confronted with civilians, defending their homeland with their blood. The Belgian government abandoned the capital, Brussels on the 17th August, and on the 20th the 3rd Uhlans were on the northern side of the city, where *Vizewachtmeister* (Probationary officer) Flume was working with his patrol, when they were ambushed by a force of Belgian infantry. It was a fearful firefight in which they had to dismount in order to fight back, and Uhlans were never as comfortable with their carbines as with their lances. Uhlan Eschoche, a brave soldier and old comrade of Flume's, got seriously wounded and they tried to get him out, but he later died of his wounds.

There had not been any official intelligence, but the Regimental records mentioned that rumours had started with the words *The English have been sighted.* Surely it was too soon for the British to have mobilized and made it to the line of battle? We need to pause, here, and look back at what was happening, not so far away; where one of history's great troop movements had been achieved, without the Germans knowing about it. The British had arrived, and were about to unleash Hell.

OVER BY CHRISTMAS

A 3rd Uhlan greets old comrades.

On the day that the 3rd Uhlans crossed the border into Belgium, the British 2nd Cavalry Brigade received orders to mobilise, at its garrison in Tidworth, the great cavalry barracks on the edge of Salisbury Plain. Among the troops were the 4th Dragoon Guards, and a certain Corporal Edward Thomas.

A British cavalry regiment had 26 officers, 523 men, 528 riding horses and 80 for support work. Headquarters employed 48 of those men, a machine-gun section of two guns had 27, and three fighting Squadrons consisted of 158 men each in four troops. The British Expeditionary Force was, indeed, terribly under-strength to meet its task, but the cavalry were unmatched in the noble blood of their horses, with whom man and beast forged legendary bonds on the polo field, in hunting and on the nation's greatest race tracks.

They started off at a shocking numerical disadvantage, having to requisition 120,000 horses at home, including any old nags they could get hold of; but the Remount Department rapidly looked for help overseas, spending over £36 million buying animals around the world, especially from the United States and Canada[23]. This would equate to £4.2 billion in 2020, which illustrates just how desperately they were needed. More than 600,000 horses and mules were shipped from North America, which included the best blood in the world, the Appaloosas. They had earned their distinction for a very good reason, having been bred expertly by the Nez Perce tribe, and put such fear into the American Army that, when crushing the tribe in 1877, they seized all the Appaloosas they could find, sold a few but slaughtered the rest in an act of butchery. They intended that these unbeatable mounts would be wiped out, to neutralise any future threat of an uprising; but a few survived – and they flourished.

The 4th Dragoon Guards mobilised rapidly and the Brigade was making its way to the Front at just about the time when the German Emperor issued a grand order to his entire armies who were now about to engage the British forces:

It is my Royal and Imperial command that you concentrate your energies, for the immediate present, upon one single purpose, and that is that you address all your skill and all the valour of my soldiers to exterminate first, the treacherous English, and walk over General French's insignificant little Army.

A British translator incorrectly wrote *contemptible* for *insignificant*, which somehow appealed to the sardonic humour of the men of the British Expeditionary Force; and the name stuck.

Whatever bold speeches the Kaiser made publicly, the German generals were well-briefed with intelligence reports that the British had

---

[23] www.nam.ac.uk/explore/british-army-horses-during-first-world-war

transformed their Army in recent years to become well-equipped, disciplined, self-confident troops. The German officers had surely to push their troops faster if there were to be any hope of following their strategy for taking Paris, but the condition that the men were in was giving cause for concern, faced with the prospect of a whole Army of fresh French troops to support the defenders. The French still showed them their backs though, and Otto's Regiment saw their armies push towards Paris with such success that, despite their fatigue, they seemed to be unstoppable.

The French thought so too. Proud French Regiments, from the socially élite cavalry guardsmen whose great-grandfathers had charged at Austerlitz, to the foot-sloggers who had tasted the world's dust from Morocco to China, had thrown themselves into the conflict, bursting with morale and revenge for the agony of 1871. Amid the atmosphere of the Belle Epoch, they all nodded sagely when Foch said, *A battle cannot be lost physically, therefore it can only be lost morally.* The French still believed that élan and naked aggression would conquer cold, military efficiency and courageous young officers, whose *ésprit* owed more to the verve of Parisian night-life than it did to modern military learning, suddenly found themselves trying to stop the world's greatest military machine with valour - and blood.

In a matter of days the negligence of the pompous French High Command had become all too clear; still, Frenchmen rallied to the call to arms, conscripts, reservists and old men, but still determined that if they were to die they would sell themselves dearly to protect their beloved Paris and all that Paris meant to them - and their officers still considered it chic to die wearing white gloves. On the Eastern Front the Russians gallantly threw in all their troops before they were fully mobilised, marching light and going into action before they were ready, to force the attention of the German High Command and thus take some pressure off the French.

The sheer strength of the German advance shocked, almost blinded, the French Army, which fell back before it, but surprise was not going to be a malady unique to the French. The Germans simply had not understood the effect that modern technology would have on firepower, making it even more vital to win victory in the first shock of attack, or else they would have no choice but to dig in - and a long drawn-out war had no place in their strategy. But the lightning attack was being slowed down because of the deadliness of the French firepower.

In the first week of the war six members of Otto's Regiment were dead, including the sorely-missed veterinary staff officer, Georg Herffurth, at Haelen on the 12th August, when the Uhlans, penetrating towards Louvain, were held up at a bridge by the massed fire of brave Belgian cavalry who had an outstanding commander, General de Witte. A rare figure among any European Army, de Witte had the wisdom to learn from recent history, using his cavalry troopers as dismounted riflemen – the mounted infantry that the British found so effective in the Boer War, and so inexplicably had abandoned them by 1914. He scored a famous victory, throwing back the German advance, and costing Otto's Regiment heavy casualties, with Uhlans laying all over the battlefield, including Georg Herffurth, who had been a distinguished officer; his death was a serious blow to the stretched resources of the Regimental staff in keeping the 3rd Uhlans fit for duty, but fit they had to be. Moreover, the number of non-fatal casualties was a constant worry: not only would they damage the strength of the team by their own loss, but they would need fit hands to carry them away from the Front Line, using up the time of valuable resources.

The Belgians were ecstatic over their victory at Haelen, persuading each other that their great fortresses protecting Liège would withstand any German assault, turning the invaders back to their Hun homeland. But on the same day, the 12th August, the great German siege guns were brought to bear upon the Belgian forts. Liège held up the German advance by two days.

But by then, that vital time upon which Germany had depended, for advancing without concerted Allied opposition, ran out. The British 2nd Cavalry Brigade arrived, covering the Expeditionary Force as it was forming up in position and concentrated around Maubeuge and Le Cateau on the left of the French Fifth Army, to advance to Mons, the regional centre of a heavy mining and engineering industry. The landscape was gently hilly but distinctly unlovely, mutilated with slag heaps and scarred by canals, railways and roads. By this time the largest of the mighty German armies were moving in, scything through Belgian and French opposition, and the British High Command quickly became convinced by cavalry reports, together with reports from aerial reconnaissance, that German infantry was heading on a collision course with the British Expeditionary Force at Mons.

The 4th Dragoon Guards had a long tradition to live up to. One of those mighty Regiments of horsemen which had distinguished themselves in Queen Victoria's wars from the Crimea to Egypt, they had received orders to mobilise for France and, on the 15th August 1914, 24 officers, 524 men and 608 horses sailed from Southampton, arriving at Boulogne the next day. A week later, they were pushing forward to hold a line south east of Mons. The Regiment's War Diary reported that, on the 21st August, patrols from C Squadron under Lieutenants Jones and Albright reported sighting the incredible number of *2,500 hostile cavalry at Soignies*[24]. So, it was, that, early next

---

[24] WO 95/1112/1

morning, Major Tom Bridges took C Squadron forward towards Casteau, where, suddenly, a troop of the 2nd Kurassiers was seen advancing along a highway when, *on seeing some of our men they turned*[25].

Among the men led by Major Brookes was Corporal Thomas. He was a Londoner, who had joined the Army as a kettle drummer in the Royal Horse Artillery but, perhaps with some awareness of his Irish ancestry, he transferred to the 4th Royal Irish Dragoon Guards before the war started. This morning he was leading his party of troopers as their Corporal, when he opened fire on the German Kurassiers; he was uncertain whether he killed or wounded the German soldier that he hit, but that was somewhat lost in the enormity of the bigger picture, for Corporal Thomas had become the first British soldier to fire a shot in anger on Continental soil since the Battle of Waterloo[26].

Meanwhile, Captain Hornby and his troopers from C Squadron galloped off in hot pursuit of the Germans and *the leading troop got in well with the sword.* They overtook eight troopers and took them prisoner, and tried to catch up with the rest, but the Germans were racing for the cover of their own infantry lines, who had dug in hasty entrenchments, and the British troopers withdrew to Obourg. In this first engagement of the war, two horses were killed and three wounded, with *Private Paget grazed in two places.* In all the best traditions of the cavalry, Captain Hornby returned to his commanding officer with his sword at the 'present', covered in German blood. Oh, the glorious war they were going to have.

---

[25] The words of Major Bridges in the Regiment's War Diary.

[26] Corporal Thomas was promoted to Sergeant on the 5th November 1915 and transferred to the Machine Gun Corps in 1916. He survived the war, having been Mentioned in Despatches for bravery and, later, earning the Military Medal.

The next morning, Sunday, the 23rd August, was shrouded in mist and rain, which cleared by about mid-morning. In the German camp, the Field Post brought the 3rd Uhlans' first, long-awaited letters from home. How wonderful it would have been if they had had the leisure to relax and savour them, but that day was to be a particularly busy one, for it was the day when the British and the German divisions clashed at the Battle of Mons.

At about 06.30 British infantry Battalions exchanged shots with German cavalry patrols, and later on their positions were 'softened up' by German artillery, a euphemism of military jargon if ever there was one. Then, at about 09.00, the men of the Middlesex Regiment first saw the German infantry advance. The Germans initially reeled from the British infantry's rapid rifle fire, which had been learned in those year-long training cycles that culminated in annual manoeuvres, and now gave them a firepower which had been hitherto unwitnessed and unknown in European conscript armies. Then the German artillery batteries pinpointed the British infantry positions and all hell let loose.

The carnage took everybody by surprise: never had such unbelievable fury of destruction been set loose on humanity. The vision of the Angel of Mons is a story that has passed into legend, but survivors swore to seeing the Angel over the battle ground, as if protecting the retreating British soldiers. As the battle raged, Otto's Regiment was deployed on the right flank as reserve cavalry, and he would have been able to see the full horror of the new age of warfare, as the full might of the German Army concentrated on the British infantry thinly spread along the canal. After the German heavy guns pounded the Middlesexes and Royal Fusiliers, German infantry attacks opened up from across the canal and increased in strength all around the salient from Obourg to Nimy. The attack spread gradually westwards along the canal and, gradually the Germans advanced to within 200 yards of the bridge at

Lock 2, where they were brought to a standstill by the accuracy of the British fire.

Still further west, the Brandenburg Grenadiers fought forward through Tertre and were only stopped by the maze of wire fences, boggy dykes and the crossfire of the West Kents and Scottish Borderers on the canal bank. By mid-day, fighting was continuous and, under continuous shelling and infantry attacks, the Battalions to the west began to fall back in the early afternoon. Near Frameries, two of the three bridges escaped being blown by lack of detonators to fire the charges, and the Germans crossed hard on the heels of the Scots Fusiliers.

As the Germans clashed with British troops, the rifle fire of the Tommies was so intense that the Germans thought they were facing lines of machine guns. Remember, that the lads of the British Expeditionary Force were professional soldiers, many of whom were veterans who had fought and won the South African War, in which the Kaiser had armed the Boers with modern artillery. These British were tough, professional, disciplined fighters, armed with state-of-the-art technology, trained better than anywhere else in Europe, and they stunned the German High Command with their bitter resistance. It was a taste of what was to come.

The Germans had learned by their recent experience, and now abandoned massed formations, deploying in extended order, as the Uhlans worked menacingly ahead of them, in reconnaissance patterns that covered the advance with ruthless efficiency. Some small parties of British troops, either not receiving orders to withdraw, or ordered to defend to the last man, were engulfed as the Germans swarmed across the canal salient, through Nimy and along the straight road into the town. The British General Staff tried to co-ordinate the withdrawal to the planned defence line, but communication had completely broken down, and parties of infantry began to get mixed up; command devolved onto captains, until they were killed, and then to lieutenants, until they were killed, then to sergeants and corporals. Worse still, though, the French retreated in chaos, and British cavalry reported getting sandwiched hopelessly between the French 1st and 2nd Divisions that had choked the roads.

The Germans did not exploit their success in the canal salient as dusk fell, and the British heard the German buglers sound the *cease fire*. It is not clear what held the Germans back from pressing their advance, but the ears of the German soldiers were ringing with praise for their great victories over the massive Allied armies. The old campaigners were not so naïve, though; they realised that such famous victories should be bringing them massive numbers of prisoners, but where were they? Nobody had seen anything but a trickle. It is not much of a victory if the enemy gets to hit back at you another day, a day when there will be fewer of you, and those left will be more tired and hungrier, than they were today. Their general, Moltke, was thinking the same thing.

Amidst all this, what about the home fires? However the professional Regulars in the British Expeditionary Force felt about the fighting, the normative ethics of Society at home would drive the momentum of the war effort, and the patriotic fervour of friends and families has passed into the history books as a defining feature of the war.

But is this the true picture? It had been less than three weeks since the British High Command had rushed to mobilise and get the Expeditionary Force to France, to share in some glory before it was all over and the Kaiser licked. Whether or not anybody had really wanted it, the whole of Europe was at war. There was no marketplace left in Europe, and the whole of Britain's peace-time trade suddenly broke down, indeed following hard on the heels of a financial crisis that has now been forgotten. Thousands of businesses were suddenly out of work, for with no trade, there was nothing for them to do. There was no such thing as state benefit of course, and therefore much of the skilled labour that industry would need for the war effort, enlisted in the Army rather than put themselves and their families through the misery and hardship of unemployment. The million volunteers were found not quite so much for their glowing hearts but for their need to earn a wage. But nobody had appreciated the damage to the war effort when, by October 1914, 12 per cent of the engineering trade had disappeared from Britain's factory floors. Without doubt, though, many young men were persuaded patriotically to volunteer for the Front, and the advantage of assured employment in the Army was merely icing on the cake. Still, whether old campaigner, unemployed worker or volunteer, what did it matter? It would all be over by Christmas.

The reality at the Front was grinding both sides down. Day by day, relentlessly, the retreating Tommies of the British Expeditionary Force were hotly pursued by the German Army. The 4th Dragoon Guards were riding in column, going to water the horses, when they heard rifle fire from the northwest side of the town of Elouges. The Colonel recorded what happened in the Regiment's War Diary in a style exactly the same as that of Colonel von Linsingen who wrote in the Diary of the 3rd Uhlans.

I received verbal orders from the Brigade Staff to gallop my Regiment and to be prepared for a determined infantry attack. I had previously been informed that one Regiment of 2nd Cavalry Brigade was holding the north and northeast of the town and I understood that the outskirts of the village were secured.

I led my Regiment along a narrow lane between a wall and high banks and was met by some rifle fire. I gave orders for the cottages to be seized to cover the exit of the lane. 2 troops of B Squadron went forward but were swept off by heavy rifle fire and shell fire. Major Bridges DSO then led a troop of his Squadron to the cottages. His horse was shot under him and he was mistakenly ridden over by his own troops in the thick dust.

We held on to the position with a few men under a very hot fire during the entire action. In order to help Major Bridges I ordered Major Hunter to take up a position but owing to extremely severe rifle and shell fire the Squadron had to withdraw to the right flank.

The machine guns were in action at the head of the lane range about 1,500 yards. The Squadron had become separated and no further concentration was possible. The order was received to withdraw to the south of the village, which was carried out without much further loss. Our casualties amounted to 81. These practically all occurred during the advance to secure a position. All officers and men behaved with great gallantry and coolness being subject for the first time in the campaign to an exceptionally heavy rifle and shell fire.

Meanwhile, the pressure on the German advance was taking its toll on their own men; the War Diary of the 3rd Uhlans recalled that the early hours of the 25th August had given no peace to them, either, as, from 01.00 they were ordered to 'make ready' and be on standby for 02.30 at the very head of the German advance. In the all-too-familiar routine now, the lancers were in the saddle again, resuming their pursuit; the 4th Squadron, Otto's Squadron, under *Rittmeister* von Stranz, was in the vanguard as they advanced along the line Somain - Mastaing - Bouchain, as far as Hordain to the east. The Regiment advanced in divisional formation to take its targets at Avesnes, Le Sec and Villers. Two Squadrons were ordered to cover Count von der Marwitz, the 1st Squadron protecting the right flank, but as they passed through

Bouchain and the area to the east of Hordain was in reach, they heard noises of battle ahead of them.

The 1st Life Hussars had stumbled into the French and found themselves in deep trouble, so the 2nd Squadron of Otto's Regiment was sent to their rescue, with orders to throw the French back. This was the first day in the war that the division advanced together in open order across country, having always been in marching column before; some freedom at last! The advanced guard pushed into St Hilaire with an attack that cut a pathway free for the advancing Army; it was a heavy struggle that lasted the afternoon, so when the town was theirs, they decided to bivouac there for the night. That evening, von Linsingen wrote in his diary:

In Bevillers we should have made bivouac, but it was still strongly occupied and so we went back to St Hilaire Les Cambrai, and found some shelter in a ruined factory.

As they looked around them, though, they saw how dreadful the place looked. In the houses and on the streets, corpses still lay around. Two Squadrons of the 2nd Dragoons who had attacked the town had suffered particularly heavy casualties, which made it all the worse. von Linsingen continued:

My Uhlans took a French general prisoner nearby and brought him to me; we could not give him anything to eat or drink, though, because we did not have anything ourselves. I showed him where to rest for the night, between me and the Adjutant, von Prittwitz and next morning I delivered him to the general on the brigade staff.

They were not to know it, but it was about this time, when the 3rd Uhlans found themselves in the same skirmish as the men of the British Hampshire Regiment. Famously nicknamed in the annals of Redcoats as The Tigers[27], they had moved up alongside the corps that had been marching ahead of them, when it had become clear that the disorganised and exhausted units would be overwhelmed if this headlong retreat could not be covered. Here, at Le Cateau, they had to make a fight of it, to give some space to enable the rest of the Expeditionary Force to disengage and fall back towards the south, in as much order as possible, even though they were overwhelmingly outnumbered by the Germans. Slowly, brutishly, exhausted companies of Tigers were being pushed back towards Solemes.

As the Battalion tried to find some defensive ground, they moved into position where the railway line passed to the south of Cattenières, when the Germans moved towards them. D company engaged them and then withdrew, before B company followed. This was the way it was going to be for the next, desperate hours. In the words of the Battalion's War Diary: *Gradually German infantry, or dismounted cavalry, appeared on our front and flanks at about 1,500 yards, and opened a desultory fire.*[28] In his very unofficial private diary, Private Pattenden of the Hampshire Regiment wrote in his personal diary[29]:

We are having our baptism of fire. We began fighting at 5.00am. It is fearful and we have a few wounded, the shrapnel shell is the chief cause.... Still fighting hard, our guns have silenced the enemy for a while. We are now waiting for the 10th and 12th Brigades to support us. The noise at times is fearful. We marvellously escaped annihilation, we had to retire and they caught us with shrapnel, it was nearly a wholescale rout and slaughter. Poor old Kennard is dead.

---

[27] They were awarded the badge of the Bengal Tiger for an incredible tour of uninterrupted service in India

[28] War diaries at the National Archives are classified under WO 95/1-3154, WO 95/3911-4193 and WO 95/5500

[29] WO 95/1495

Fascinatingly, we have a view of the skirmish, running at the same time from the other side. From the Regimental diary, the picture emerged that they were woken at 04.30 in their ground bivouacs, still exhausted after a night's rest that was all too short. The Army's logistics had failed so badly that all they could have for breakfast was coffee - not even any bread to go with it. Intelligence reports affirmed that the Allied enemy was camped between Maubeuge and Givet, Namur had fallen and the 5th Army was also in a triumphant advance but the advance was still badly delayed. The 5th Cavalry Brigade, forming the advanced guard of the whole German Army, struck camp swiftly to operate that day with Jäger Battalions 4, 7 and 9. Their mission that day was to push beyond Solemes and cross the main highway half-way between Cambrai and Le Cateau, heading south-west, to that modest little town called Cattenières; then they would swing west for the Bapaume road, and head south for Peronne.

Soon they had reached the railway station on the south side of Cattenières, but then they ran into deep trouble, for on the heights just north of Longsart was a strong British fortified redoubt, and beyond that were columns of troops – it was, of course, the Tigers that they were facing. A member of Otto's Regiment wrote words that later found their way into the Regimental Diary:

Towards 7.00am our advanced guard was fighting for its life. Then the Division orderly officer, Lt Colonel von Kleist, the darling of the Regiment (he later died a fine soldier's death in Russia) galloped up and brought the news: "In front of us are the English. The 5th Cavalry Brigade are all going to be riflemen."

The problem was that this was no job for horsemen; they had to dismount and attack as infantry.

Machine Gun Detachment No 4 under Captain Albrich at once took up position and trained fire on the whole enemy front. Meanwhile, the mounted machine gun detachment on wagons set off as fast as possible around both sides of Cattenières, while the riflemen together with Jäger Battalions 4 and 7 halted the enemy division in the streets. The 3rd Uhlans and 2nd Dragoons, making up the 5th Cavalry Brigade fought on foot with their carbines, over the railway tracks on the west with Jäger Battalion No 7 on the right flank in the direction of Longsart, while the other part of the division proceeded from the station to the south.

This was tough, deadly work and quite different to the dashing operations to which light cavalry aspired. The Jägers, though, were seasoned foot-soldiers and used to just this sort of job, specialising in the crafts of extended cover and scouting. Named after the German word for a hunter, Jägers were still trained on the principles that Frederick the Great had declared, *so that when the Army advances or a detachment is sent out, the troops may be reliable guides who know all the passages and roads.* They worked hand in hand with the cavalry, and they achieved results; now they were all needed.

Colonel von Arnim, Otto's Brigade Commander and a famous son of Silesia, had brought the leaders of his strike force to Cattenières and they made their base at the railway station. Hardly had his troops crossed the tracks when they got caught right in the hellish firing line of hardened Tommies of the Hampshire Regiment. As the Lancashires strode north from Longsart to take the Germans head on, the Tigers of the Hampshire Regiment rushed out in extended formation from the south-east, straight into the 2nd Dragoons on the German left flank. The Dragoons were lying flat in a field of beetroot and the Tigers had not seen them, when they opened fire at close range, and they took the British by surprise as bullets whistled past their ears. After a short pause for breath, the Germans sprang forward and soon the khaki uniforms of the British were completely overwhelmed by the Division's fast advance as they searched for a position to dig in.

The British threw in their reserves under a covering fire and it was a bloody fight before they were pushed back at about 14.00 when their first position was taken as the German riflemen stood, unprotected, firing at the line of retreating British infantry. The 2nd Squadron of Otto's Regiment took 50 prisoners back with them that day. The other Squadrons of the Regiment did not want to stay the night there and, burning with victory, seized the opportunity to pursue the fleeing British, until halted by covering British heavy artillery fire.

In the Headquarters of the British 4th Division, a staff officer gathered all the intelligence he could on the fight at Cattenières, reporting that the 2nd Cavalry Division, accompanied by the Jäger Battalion, *held a position today along the railway embankment near Cattenières against a British force superior in numbers.* Meanwhile, on the other side of the lines, they were tasting the bittersweet rewards of war. The Regimental record put it strongly, that, in the day of the heaviest fighting so far, Otto and his comrades had the British soundly on the run. Then they counted up the cost. Five troopers, three NCOs and one officer were dead, 21 were wounded and 9 missing. They were lucky: Jäger Battalion No 4 left 28 dead at Cattenières.

Wearily, thankfully, Otto and his comrades fell into their bivouacs that night and slept a dead sleep; a glance at the map will show graphically the incredible amount of ground they were covering, in constant danger. Yet again, their rest was all too short, for the next morning the advance had to continue. The Regiment was the first on the road from Cambrai to Bapaume, names that would become passionate metaphors for the horrors of war. As the vanguard unit they rode hard to Velu on the Sailly road. *Leutnant* von Klinkowström and his patrol of ten Uhlans was followed by *Leutnant* von Stutterheim some three to five hundred paces behind.

Before reaching the town of Barastre they met a patrol from the 12th Dragoons who said that there were two French cavalry Squadrons in the town of Rocquiny. On the other side of Barastre they left the road and rode across country to Sailly. Just 700 to 800 metres further on they discovered three French cavalrymen behind some sheaves of corn. Deciding to move stealthily around them and take them prisoner, *Leutnant* von Klinkowström and his ten troopers rode around to the right to trap them. The French cavalry were out on a limb and the Germans were keen to attack, so the Uhlans committed themselves. But when they were two hundred metres away, 16 French cavalry appeared.

The Regimental record reported what happened next in a blow-by-blow account. From a distance of just 30 metres *Leutnant* von Klinkowström yelled, *Hurrah for an Uhlan's death!* At the same moment the French saw them and wheeled to the right in order to avoid the front of the German attack. The Uhlans swung round to the left to pursue them, but during the turn von Klinkowström lost his Luger pistol. After a 500-metre gallop they caught up with the trailing Frenchmen and a tough struggle followed as the Prussians took two troopers prisoner and killed twelve. The French officer was way ahead of them, though, anxious to avoid sharing the same fate as the rest of his patrol. A French trooper had been thrown from his horse and tried to fire at them. At once two Uhlans sprang from their horses to deal with the enemy horseman in a manner appropriate to a short, sharp war.

This was what they had come for; and, for all the action, the Regiment did not suffer a single death that day. Darkness had fallen by 22.00 when they reached Moislains, north of Peronne, having spearheaded the reconnaissance for the Army's advance towards Paris; job well done, they decided to bivouac at Moislains for the night. The fateful name of that town would stay in the memory of every member of the Regiment. Perhaps, as they relaxed with a bottle of liberated brandy, they shared their experiences of the day, reckoning up the British whose cavalry culture they once admired but who now clashed head-on with the realities of the twentieth century. It was a shared experience.

Fighting alongside the 4th Dragoon Guards were the 9th Lancers, led by one David Graham Muschet Campbell, known to his friends as 'Soarer'. He had been commissioned into the Regiment in 1889, and his career path followed that of many a cavalry subaltern, as he carved his reputation - not as a soldier, but as a steeplechaser, winning everything from the Irish National Hunt Cup to the Grand National. In March 1912 he was appointed Officer Commanding the 9th Lancers and, under his leadership, they became one of the foremost Regiments in the British cavalry. For some in the High Command, Campbell was not their favourite son, for he had harnessed his intelligence to his personal experience, and championed initiative and new ideas which defied the old cavalry traditions. As a result, he had already earned a reputation for criticising orders which he believed to be wrong or inconsistent with modern warfare. But he was an excellent soldier, and knew his duty, whether or not he agreed with the donkeys in the brass hats.

Just the day before yesterday, nine German gun batteries were pounding the British withdrawal. They had been cleverly placed on the other side of a sugar refinery, and protected from counter-attack by slag heaps, railway lines, sunken roads - and plain, barbed wire fences. The commander of the 2nd Cavalry Brigade sent the 4th Dragoon Guards and 9th Lancers to give the batteries a taste of cold steel with a classic cavalry charge. But Soarer Campbell was not happy.

More of a disciple of the yeomanry tactics of mounted infantry,

Campbell would have preferred to gallop forward and then fight dismounted, making the best use of ground – but this time he had no choice. As the cavalry advanced down the sunken lane towards its target, he led from the front - in fact, very far in front, for, as his horse, Crasher, galloped towards the Germans, he found himself nearly a hundred yards in front of the rest of the Regiment, facing a phalanx of German lancers. Amazingly, he survived, despite twice being wounded, as his cavalry charged down the narrow lane at the gallop towards the German position. The style was Napoleonic, and stood no chance in the twentieth century, facing a hail of shelling, machine gun fire and rifle fire. Most ignobly of all, though, the entire charge was brought to a dead stop by a simple barbed wire fence – just as the German cavalry had discovered as well. Campbell's Squadron Commander, Francis Grenfell, spoke just as well for the Uhlans when he said:

We had simply galloped like rabbits in front of a line of guns.

For their part, the Tommies in the ranks of the Hampshire Regiment marched, and marched, slogging across country for four hours solid with hardly a break. They marched all day, they marched all night, before they reached Ham at 07.00 on the 28th August. Out of a Battalion of a thousand men, there were 100 men left in the Hampshires, who had met up with 150 of the Rifle Brigade and East Lancashires. The Hampshire Regiment's War Diary reported the situation bluntly:

As far as we knew, these were the sole survivors of the 11th Infantry Brigade. After an hour's halt at Ham we pushed on steadily all day, 15 miles of hilly road, through Hoyon to Sempigny. It was intensely hot and we were pursued all day by the sound of guns behind us. At 5.30am we halted, absolutely dead beat, but were assisted by Royal Army Medical Corps and Royal Engineers units who had arrived there previously, and cooked stews for the troops as they arrived. Our 1st and 2nd line transport also met us at this bivouac where we stayed nearly 24 hours and got the first rest and hot meal we had had since we left the train.

Private Pattenden of the Hampshire Regiment wrote down his own feelings on the 28th in his personal diary:

My God, the battle is raging again here now, when will it end. I am far too full for words or speech and feel paralysed as this affair is now turning into a horrible slaughter.

So how fared the men who were wounded? Sited as near as possible to the fighting was the Regimental Aid Post, manned by the Battalion Medical Officer, supported by his stretcher bearers and orderlies. A very quick analysis would be made, and the wounded man sent back by field ambulance to an Advanced Dressing Station, still close to the front line but better equipped to deal with the wounded than the RAP. Here the wounds would be dressed, and some emergency operations carried out. But right now, at the height of August's fighting, the advanced dressing stations were drowning in the tidal wave of casualties in this mass carnage, and wounded men might be lying, dying, waiting for attention, for an age, and by the wagonload.

From here, the wounded would be taken to the Casualty Clearing Station, or Clearing Hospital, as they were known then. This was a tented camp, but nevertheless well-equipped for conducting serious operations such as amputations, where the cases too serious to travel further were cared for; minor cases were treated and returned to the front line, and all the others were evacuated to the great military hospitals back home. More than half the casualties were sent back, by ambulance train and hospital ship, to these General Hospitals. And the front line, of course, was forever being pushed back. Even amidst such pressure, the British medical teams were forbidden by the Geneva

Convention from prioritising Allied wounded over German ones. Yet, there appears scant evidence that British wounded resented the treatment of German prisoners. Indeed, evidence throughout the war suggests that the British Tommy in the field respected his wounded German counterpart.

Major A C Priestley of the Royal Army Medical Corps was at the very centre of it all when the British captured the town of Landrecies. The horrifying torrent of wounded needed immediate attention and so they had to improvise:

After capture, the boys' school in Landrecies was converted into an emergency hospital for the shelter of our wounded.

We found Number 4 Field Ambulance in possession of the girls' school, and the military hospital with many severely wounded.

After staying there a few days all the ambulance waggons were loaded with cases fit for transport, and taken by the Germans, with practically the whole medical personnel, by road to Mons.

Captain Egan, RAMC, and myself were left behind with about 40 to 50 cases unfit for transport. With us were left sufficient rank and file to nurse the wounded.

I collected the wounded left behind from the various buildings, and brought them all into one building, the Ecole des Filles, as being the most suitable.

While here we lost a few cases, some dying from tetanus. Records were kept of all cases in hospital, and pay books, and identification tallies, carefully collected. The dead were buried in the churchyard.

The mayor and villagers gave every assistance, the tradespeople giving bread and meat, the chemists drugs etc, on requisition.

The Germans rapidly overwhelmed the position, of course, but they did not interfere with this makeshift military hospital too much, allowing them to get on with their work. So, some days later:

The wounded were now progressing well, so Captain Egan and I decided that one of us should make an attempt to rejoin our Army.

It was decided that I should remain with the wounded, as I had a better knowledge of languages, which was useful when requisitioning food and drugs. Captain Egan left. I was in Landrecies about three weeks, during which time I acted as medical officer to the civil population, and was able to bring in several wounded British soldiers who were in hiding in the surrounding country.

Otto's Regiment had rested overnight in Moislains, and at about 09.00 on the 28th, they were busy on forage duties and had not formed up. Their exhaustion was now so great that they had forgotten a golden rule of warfare respected since ancient times: they had ill-protected themselves against a surprise attack, no doubt relying on the heavy fog to protect them while it also hindered their reconnaissance duties. Suddenly they came under heavy attack from the French 61st and 62nd Reserve Divisions.

In its bivouac at the northern entrance to Moislains, the Regiment took the first impact of the British attack. It was up to them to protect the temporary, vulnerable position where the division had camped. There was instant chaos as they tried to rally together in the fog, and in such a serious crisis it was only the outstanding behaviour of the commander and his team that prevented panic from breaking out; if it had, they would have been lost.

The place where the Regiment had bivouacked was at the foot of a small rise in the ground, from behind which the British infantry fire was concentrated, and the bullets whistled right over their heads, but actually did little harm. But it was very clear that the British would completely overrun their position in no time, unless they very swiftly formed an effective resistance. They were dismounted, of course, so all the Uhlans had with which to fight back were their carbines. They had not had any time to dress, and most of them were wearing only their shirts and trousers. With admirable guts the Uhlans fought back, without thinking of the cost, in an incredibly bitter fire-fight with the French infantry.

The fog had lifted and turned the morning into a bright summer's day, in which Uhlans had to do their duty or die. The fighting was furious but the 3rd Uhlans stood firm, until the dragoons and hussars arrived to the aid of Otto and his comrades. Together they pressed the British - the vanguard Battalion, the crème, of an infantry brigade - back into retreat. It was a remarkable testimony to the bravery and determination of disciplined men, armed only with carbines against trained British infantry well-armed with rifles before they could recover their trusty, beloved horses to fight back and repel their assailants.

But what was the price of their survival? 27 men from the 3rd Uhlans died that day; 49 were wounded and 9 missing. Even *Leutnant* Freiherr von Richthofen was slightly wounded. To give an idea of how appalling these casualty figures were, one should compare these losses with those suffered in the Charge of the Light Brigade sixty years previously, when the news so shocked the British people at home to hear that the Regiment which suffered the heaviest casualties lost 24 men dead, 37 wounded and 14 taken prisoner; then the Brigade's commander, Lord Cardigan, retired to his yacht to consume a bottle of champagne. Most soberingly of all, compared with some Regiments, the 3rd Uhlans were doing well right now: rumours were going round that some infantry Regiments had been wiped out.

For the Regiment, it had been a day of crushing emotion which ended in utter exhaustion. Otto's commander, Colonel von Linsingen, tried to write brave words in the diary: how the French territorial infantry attacked them and took them by surprise; how most of the troopers were in the town at the time, foraging for food and water for the horses when they had to rally and beat the French back to win the day. Reading between the lines, though, one somehow gets the impression that they did not feel very victorious, just exhausted, and that if the battle had gone the other way they could at least say that they had done their duty.

In two days the Regiment had lost two officers dead, Ensign August von Hellfeld at Cattenières on the 26th, and Ensign Ernst Frankenberg-Luttiss, on the 28th at Moislains. These promising young officers were really boys in men's clothing, but the troopers and non-commissioned officers who failed to answer their names at roll-call would prove the heaviest loss to try to make up and the extra burden would have to be shared by all. For Otto, it meant extra responsibilities on badly-fed, badly-rested shoulders.

The Regiment still had to maintain the pace at all costs and on the 29th August the march to Paris was pressed as hard as ever; it had to, if their objective of taking the Capital had any chance of success, but they also knew that, although the odds were shortening against them, failure in this task could land them all in serious risk of their lives.

During the day they met up with their old comrades from happier days on manoeuvres, the 12th Grenadier Regiment, to discover that they had suffered such heavy casualties during fighting in which they had distinguished themselves that they had won the special distinction of the highest warriors in their division[30]. Otto and his comrades would have congratulated them warmly, but they knew that their words sounded hollow because of the appalling casualties suffered in just these first few weeks and already it was becoming clear that some very senior strategists in the High Command had missed a most important factor: they had forgotten the impact of modern technology on warfare and the whole affair was becoming very grim.

It was to become grimmer still. Otto was serving on the right wing of the German advance, which, under the Schlieffen Plan, was virtually to circumvent Paris and take the Capital from the south-west. In order to achieve this, Schlieffen had stipulated that the right flank had to be eight times stronger than the left flank. The Kaiser's executive commander, von Moltke, had departed from Schlieffen's plan, though. He had already been lumbered with the legacy of Italy's neutrality. Schlieffen had depended on the support of those five Italian Army corps to support the German advance, but with Italy's withdrawal from the Triple Alliance, they never materialised. Then Moltke sent six reserve divisions to support the 6th Army in Lorraine. In effect, Moltke left himself with his crucial right flank only three times the size of the left - a fraction of that demanded in Schlieffen's plan - but it still had to achieve its original objective. Its weakness was shown up badly against the resistance of the French and British forces, with the result that time was running out for the German strategy, and Moltke lost his nerve: in a dramatic departure from the Schlieffen Plan, Otto received new orders that they must now swing south to take Paris from the east. It was a decision that would leave a gap of 48 kilometres

---

[30] One of the most illuminating accounts of the war from the German perspective has been given by an officer from this Regiment. See Bloem, W, 2011 (reprint), The Advance from Mons 1914: The Experiences of a German Infantry Officer, Helion & Company Ltd

between the armies of Kluck and Below, ignoring a cardinal rule of warfare - never divide your forces.

When Moltke saw the danger, he ordered Kluck to change direction and follow in echelon behind Below's 2nd Army. But Kluck refused; he was convinced that, if there were strong forces in Paris, they would still only be assembling; it was crucial to press on with the advance to cross the Marne, and attack Paris before the defenders were ready. Once Paris fell, the war would be over. Very possibly, he was right. But that gap between the two armies would have untold consequences.

On the 30th August, the German Army made a push against the right flank of the strong French division of General d'Amade's Territorials at Amiens, the old capital of Picardy on the fateful river Somme, and forced the defenders back, holding the advance on the line Moreuil - Roye. But every step forward was now proving more difficult, as the French had learnt their lessons well. Slowing down the German advance daily, they made good use of ground features, like trees and bushes. They put out small observation posts everywhere and gave them completely covered fire positions. Their machine guns were often posted in batteries in the upper stories of houses, giving the best possible range of fire, and you could tell at once friend from foe as the French machine guns had a slower, rat-tat rate of fire. Against this bitter, dogged, life-or-death defence, Otto reconnoitred the line Noyon - Compiegne and the Allied enemy left flank against a possible counter-attack from the Oise. It was a long and difficult day, as their advance was being slowed down by Allied enemy resistance, who were making the most of the deadly cover provided by the great forests to the east of the road to Compiegne. They spent the night, exhausted, in Solente, once again without finding anything to eat.

The next day the advance guard carried on, reconnoitring the ground that would take them to Paris, going ahead of the Army across the Oise and over the Noyon - Compiegne line, as the right flank of the Army made a forced march to reach the Maignelay line, with their left wing on the Aisne - Epagny line. It was the last day of the month in which they had gone to war; an exciting month for them all, that had seen a huge achievement by Otto and the advance troops of the German Army; but the casualty lists had been shocking. Carefully-calculated German statistics could not get the figures below 1,458 German dead with total casualties of 9,213.

These were fearful losses, especially for the period of the war when it was anticipated that the lightning attack on Paris would have minimised casualties, and the commanders at the Front had been reporting dramatic victories to Berlin. But already it was clear that modern warfare in a Europe of sophisticated technology involved nightmarish wastage that simply could not be sustained if the war were to remain a highly mobile one. The good news was that now they really were getting close to their goal; the deadly encirclement of Paris and the coup de grace to the French Army from the rear was still on the cards. The endless waves of *feldgrau* uniforms were pushing the British and French armies back all the time, but their exhaustion was ever-present, afflicting every man as sure as a disease.

A German soldier by the name of Georg Bucher survived the war to describe graphically in his own book the sights and sounds which would have been Otto's constant companion in the German lines in those first few weeks of the war, making it all the easier to step into his shoes[31]. All night, rest was almost impossible and they would bivouac as best they could. There was not even any question of burying their dead. Occasional shells would pass over, now from one side, now from the other. Verey lights sent up flares all night to illuminate the

---

[31] Bucher, G, 2006 (reprint), In the Line, Naval & Military Press

battlefield, as horse artillery clattered by and in the ruddy glow of the lamps on the ammunition wagons, Otto could see the field grey uniforms, hear the jingle of harness, the curses and ahead of them a sharp command, *Halt - keep to the right*. Ambulances would pass by, bumping hard on their springs along the rough road. From one of the ambulances would come a cry, *O God ... O God ... O God.*

The state of the German troops did not seem to be particularly weak to the British and French forces trying vainly, desperately, to halt their advance. The British Commander in Chief, Sir John French, was alarmed at the continuous changes in the battle plans. The French High Command was anxious to make a stand now. Field Marshal French, however, wanted to study the entire question before committing himself; in the meantime his Army would continue to fall back. The Commander of the French forces, 'Papa' Joffre, could take no more. He stormed into French's headquarters:

So far as regards the French Army, my orders are given and whatever may happen I intend to throw my last company into the balance to win a victory and save France. It is in her name that I come to you to ask for British assistance, and I urge it with all the power I have in me. I cannot believe that the British Army will refuse to do its share in this supreme crisis; history would severely judge your absence.

The silence then was deafening as French stared at him. Joffre banged his fist on the table and roared:

Monsieur le Maréchal, the honour of England is at stake!

French quietly replied, *I will do all I possibly can*, and served tea. This was no time to lose one's head.

At the sharp end of the proceedings, Otto and his comrades were learning hard lessons. The first thing to do against an enemy occupying a defensive position, was to form a screen of patrols, who would ascertain how the position was occupied and where its strengths and weaknesses lay. A detail of men would skirmish with the enemy to hold them down, while the remainder would be held ready to strike the blow at the decisive point, but lines of skirmishers extended at less than two paces apart proved dangerous, because the fury of the British fire would cut them to pieces. Their patrols had been carried out in close formation as their training dictated, and inevitably they came under hails of fire, so that unnecessary casualties were being inflicted. More than that, of course, it would have been unthinkable for a proud Prussian officer, a Brandenburger at that, to duck or take cover, especially in the heat of battle, as a result of which they were losing so many highly trained officers that many units came back leaderless. They would soon have to issue orders to the proud Officer Corps of Frederick the Great that officers had to take cover in the same way as the other ranks.

Berlin: Rankstrasse in 1900. The Scholz family home is clearly visible on the left.

Berlin: Rankstrasse today. The Scholz family home has been demolished and the building is now an office of a car parking company.

Rittmeister von Roeder.

Oberlt Freiherr von Reiswiss und Kanderzin.

Rittmeister von Kuhne.

Colonel von Linsingen.

Meaux 1914: The Battle of the Marne.

Meaux 1987. The bridge was repaired and still stands.

THE BATTLE OF THE MARNE

3rd Uhlans Mounted Machine Gun Team

As the eyes and ears of the generals, Otto was busy evaluating the Allied enemy forces, identifying their strengths and their weaknesses. Already it was clear that the British made good defensive positions - hard experience had taught them that the British dug out their shallow firing trenches very quickly, before the Germans even knew that they were there, and they waited patiently in them, having measured the distances at which they could fire their rifles to the most deadly effect; so the advancing Germans did not see them until they were on top of them, when the Tommies opened a truly hellish fire on the unsuspecting cavalry.

But the Germans were learning quickly, and soon realised when British infantry was planning to counterattack, because they would see an advanced guard deploy from the front lines. It always looked a weak sort of force, covered by scouts in extended order, but it was a ruse that could trap an unwary enemy, because the main body would be deploying behind. It would look inactive for a long time, and an inexperienced young German cavalry trooper out on reconnaissance could get misled, or mightily confused. But they learned to tell soon enough when the counterattack was starting, when they saw lines of skirmishers following one another at about three hundred metres distance, advancing at wide and irregular intervals.

The tough British soldiers, battle-hardened from countless Imperial wars, had an inexhaustible initiative when it came to tactics in those early, desperate weeks of fighting. It was often an effective trick to draw the Germans into an attack by showing them just a small retiring force, so the Jägers and the Uhlans thought that they could break through there with fewer troops. All the time, though, the main body of Tommies was deploying, so once the modest German force was committed, the whole force of the British infantry fell upon them. But when they were truly defending, the British infantry reserve was always strong, and would counter-attack like lightning against the unsuspecting German flanks.

Meanwhile, a German cavalryman doing a reconnaissance of their defensive positions would watch mobile detachments, usually motor transport with machine guns or horse artillery, pushing out in front and on the flank of the true position, to outwit the Germans and induce the British infantry to deploy prematurely, and run off in the wrong direction. German intelligence officers warned their troops to pay deep respect to the British artillery, which they found to be very well-trained; they avoided long lines of guns, but fired from widely dispersed positions. Batteries usually took a long time to get into action, but then they fired very accurately. Artillery positions were some of the most vital pieces of information that a cavalryman could get for his commanders.

At 02.00 in the cold small hours of the 2nd September, the 4th Dragoon Guards received orders to turn out the guard as quickly as possible: this could only mean that reports had come in of a German attack. Two hours later they were marching as advance guard of the Brigade, and arrived at Ermenonville at about 06.00, where they received information that German guard cavalry had got around their rear. But there was a great deal of confusion to contend with, for when they arrived in the town, they found that the Germans had left in a hurry, perhaps on learning of their approach – they had even left the engines running in the support lorries that could not get out of town in time. The realisation was dawning on them that, now, the Germans were turning away from them.

It was certainly not a headlong retreat but, perhaps, some sign that the Germans were falling away from the 4th Dragoon Guards and hurriedly re-drawing their lines, maybe concentrating elsewhere to perform a sleight of hand and punch a shock attack on the strategic line that crossed the Marne, and take Paris while the Allies were still reeling. At 21.20 on the 3rd September, in his headquarters, Major H W Studd of the British General Staff finished writing his report for the day. His information was that the German 5th Cavalry Brigade had reached Chateau Thierry, Checy and Saulthey in no great strength but small forces of all arms were at each place.

The French Army is falling back tonight, he wrote, *with its left on St Barthelemy 13 miles east of La Ferté covered by cavalry. Its left will be about Rebais tomorrow night 8 miles east of La Ferté.*

The same day he had received a report that large bodies of German troops had been seen by air reconnaissance the previous night, 15 miles north-northwest of Meaux, advancing in three columns. The German advance was heading for the ancient town of Meaux, a strategic point on the main railway line to the East that made it less than an hour's journey from the centre of Paris. Now the French government abandoned Paris, heralded by a long Proclamation that verged on the Operatic; but only the first two paragraphs are necessary to sum up the French position:

PEOPLE OF FRANCE!

For several weeks relentless battles have engaged our heroic troops and the Army of the enemy. The valour of our soldiers has won for them at several points, marked advantages; but in the north the pressure of the German forces has compelled us to fall back. This situation has compelled the President of the Republic and the Government to take a painful decision.

In order to watch over the national welfare, it is the duty of the public powers to remove themselves temporarily from the city of Paris....

On the next day, the 4th September, the 3rd Uhlans had reached La Ferté sous Jouarre, the nearest large town on the road to Meaux. The River Marne flowed below them, and following the course of the river they would find the cathedral of Meaux dominating the countryside atop its hill in the town. They rode as far as La Ferté sous Jouarre, where they were halted by artillery fire. Then they swung round to La Borde[32] where they decided to bivouac for the night. Men and horses were exhausted beyond endurance; in fact, that day Kluck reported to Army High Command that his units were fast approaching collapse - but Otto and his comrades were so close to Paris now, they felt they could almost smell it in the air.

Far behind, in his headquarters, with only dim intelligence from the front, Moltke was not so happy:

---

[32] Les Bordes in the Regimental records

We must not deceive ourselves. We have had successes, but we have not had victory. When armies of millions of men are opposed, the victor has prisoners. Where are ours?

In fact, the *complete victories* that had been reported back by the Army commanders, which had led to such optimism at headquarters and rejoicing by the Kaiser, were only local gains. The British and French had controlled their retirement with skill, but now they were ready, for this was the place where the Allied armies were going to make their stand. The battle line stretched from the Dutch border and curved down past Paris to the Grand Morin, then on to the mighty fortress of Verdun where it ran into Lorraine, then south and ended at the Alps. Fourteen armies with over two million men were poised to fight for enormous stakes. Most of them had gone through the harshest baptism of fire to get there; they were veterans who were well-used to the dreadful noise that shells made as they passed overhead, the same noise, a survivor would one day observe, as a giant dog vomiting. The past month's experience had taught them those basic survival skills, such as how to judge the height and distance of incoming shells roaring overhead, so they would only have to dive down for the dangerous ones. These vital souls from the Europe of the *Belle Epoch* learned in a month to adapt to this new, high-technology war - they had to, for their daily survival.

The scene was set. The hot sun had set on yet another day of atrociously bitter warfare and the summer night sky was inky black as Otto checked the horses and then his men, before he himself could lay down, as exhausted in mind as in body, inwardly frightened but determined not to show it. It was to be his last night of freedom.

At first light on the Sabbath Day of the 6th September, the German commanding general went ahead of the troops by motor car, to reconnoitre the land from Brinches, just south of Meaux, and back towards the Marne. In the light morning mist lay the land that would soon be bitterly contested, the Marne Valley. One wonders if, that morning, Otto's mind touched briefly on memories of Sunday at home in Berlin, strolling with friends in the Tiergarten, family dinners full of happiness. But he could not have thought about it for long. At 09.20 a flight from 30 Squadron returned from a reconnaissance flight over the Ourcq, reporting:

The enemy in strength at least 1 division is going towards the line Meaux - St Pathus. The right flank is near Neufmontiers, the left is near St Pathus and with sections apparently well near Bregy. The direction of the advance of the entire enemy in east and northeasterly direction in extended formation and batteries. The main mass of the enemy is near St Soupplets.

The 2nd Division had crossed the Marne and were reconnoitring as far as Coulommiers on the Grand Morin, well south of La Ferté; and even beyond, towards Rozoy, before they swung east to Le Corbier. The 3rd Uhlans had penetrated to Pecy, where the British cavalry were reported, and the 2nd Dragoons advanced to Jouy le Chatel. Skirmishing, some Allied cavalry opened fire on the German advance guard near Rozoy, and were soon reinforced by infantry, just as a heavy artillery bombardment rained all about them. The Germans were left in no doubt that the enemy was about to launch a big counter-attack.

For the whole campaign, the men in Otto's brigade had fought on the sharp edge of the Army's most westerly flank. Now the protagonists were braced for the decisive battle that would make or break the German advance. To the readers of the world's newspapers of the time, as much as to us today, it is the broad picture of the battle that is portrayed, and the individual melts into terms of divisions, corps and armies. It is a neat, sanitised way of studying war, to look at maps with symbols of brigades and divisions and arrows pointing here and there, to read the orders of battle and move comfortably in one's chair as one embraces the finer points of the consequences of the battle. For it takes away the suffering.

Every symbol on the map represents thousands, tens of thousands of men, fighting in troops and platoons, Squadrons and companies, handfuls of men bitterly working to stay together and reach their objective, seeing the friend beside them losing his legs or his brains, desperate to keep their bearings in the confusion of battle, exhausted, tormented by lice, stinking for want of a wash, unable to relieve themselves when they needed to most in their lives.

Even then, that does no justice to the thousands of souls among the men in those symbols who suffered the horror of wounding, maiming, shattered minds. And death: for some of them, a split-second's experience in an exploding shell, for others, a long, agonised, frightful death in a shell hole or on the open ground, or on a stretcher alongside countless others at a casualty clearing station. Some of them thought of their homes in Berlin or Bristol, Munich or Montmartre; others were just in too much pain to think of anything at all. For every thousand souls there are a thousand ways of suffering.

At 06.00 the 4th Dragoon Guards marched towards the Germans, acting as advance guard for the whole Division, and C Squadron was right at the front, when they saw a large mass of German cavalry, advancing towards Jouy le Chatel. The Regiment was just about holding their ground around Percy, but got shelled out of there by German artillery. Their comrades in the 9th Lancers were sent up to support them, but the same thing happened to them; then a battery of artillery was sent to give them covering fire – but they were not needed, for the German was falling back. In his diary, Private Pattenden wrote:

6th September. 1130. For the first time we have made an advance and have come back to where we began yesterday via Gretz Ferrieres and Jossigny. There is a great battle in front of us, guns are now booming far away and we believe we hold the river against advance. It is very hot here makes our marching much harder. There is an Army corps in front of us and I suppose we shall soon begin to fight again. More heartaching foot slogging till 6 or 7 o'clock. This is the hardest part the marches and counter-marches.

By this time, the British Expeditionary Force had suffered 10 per cent casualties, but the quality of their organisation was beginning to tell, as replacements were rapidly filling the ranks, and supplies were getting through efficiently to the very front, thanks to the Quartermaster-General, Sir William Robertson. The British troops, now seasoned in the new horror, were eager to advance and make a stand of it. So it was, that after breakfast on the 6th September, for the first time, they were ordered to march in a northerly direction, instead of southerly, which gave a boost to their morale. Suddenly there was laughter and talking in the ranks, as they advanced to meet the Germans on the banks of the River Marne. They would not give any more. The clash which followed changed the tide of the war.

As the German pilots took their aircraft further over the Allied enemy lines, their observers entered on their report cards the details of the enemy infantry and artillery units below. This gave the commanders on the ground essential information, with clear pictures of the battle positions. With this information the High Command was able to identify where the enemy's strengths and weaknesses were likely to be, deciding where to direct Otto and his men to probe the lines and break through areas of resistance. Not a single soul could now surely have failed to realise how high the stakes were in this day's work, as Otto and his comrades tried to break through the enemy, to fight on to the

Capital that was now so close, and the fighting became desperate.

This time, the British and French troops were repelling them; the left wing of the Army was south of the Grand Morin, where they were in need of immediate support, but the fighting was so heavy on the right that the support could not be spared to reach them. Meanwhile, the battle on the Ourcq was raging with dreadful ferocity along the whole front. General von der Marwitz had the intelligence before him that had been gathered by the aircraft, the jägers and the cavalry, the telephone posts and the casualty stations, and by midday he had decided that the Allied enemy could not be held. At 14.00 the 2nd Cavalry Division was ordered to break off the engagement, so that they could regroup at Amillis.

Germans learned a new experience on the Marne and, maybe, it was the Allies' secret weapon. This was the weapon of Disorder; not inflicted by the British or the French, but by the Germans themselves. For effective command fell apart at the top, right at the time when it was needed most. Suddenly, Kluck was fighting his own war here, and his men - Otto and his comrades - were fighting everywhere on basic instinct. Attack was beaten off by counter-attack; amid the chaos, some pockets of men were holding, others were retreating. The whole battlefield, miles and miles of it, was a scene of bitter resistance; and all the while, slowly, but inexorably, the Allies were widening the gap that divided Kluck's and Bulow's armies, exploiting the High Command's fateful mistake of dividing its forces.

The ancient strategy of divide and conquer never goes out of fashion, and the Allies now made the most of it. Kluck saw his forces in deep trouble, and nowhere more so than in the area around La Ferté. The Allied enemy vanguard should have been stopped between Meaux and La Ferté; but it was not stopped, and was pushing harder on the banks of the Marne. The situation was so bad at La Ferté that, at 17.30, IV Corps was ordered to stand by to support the surviving forces that had pulled back to the area north of the town. This fateful stretch of land was where Otto was fighting for his life, stormed at with shot and shell while having to carry out his job of spying and observation, advanced map-reading with compass-bearings and all the calculations needed for pinpointing objects observed to an accurate map reference, so that the generals, and the artillery, could do their jobs.

Both sides knew that this was the last-ditch fight for Paris and fought all the more bitterly. It proved truly to be the most decisive day of the whole of the Great War, for on this day, the 6th September 1914, the Germans, battle-weary and exhausted from their month-long advance which nobody had predicted would be such a trial by ordeal, were finally halted, just a short drive from the goal that would have brought the war to an end and, under the pressure of the British and French armies, the mighty, magnificent, awesome, German war machine was painfully, agonisingly, pushed back. Brave men from all parts of Germany who had gone through so much to get there, would weep openly when their commanders later told them that they would after all be abandoning the march to Paris. It was a frenetic day, almost bewildering, as orders were made and changed just as rapidly on both sides. A French lieutenant of dragoons recalled:

For my part, I preserve only a confused and burning recollection of the days of the 6th and 7th September... The heat was suffocating. The exhausted troopers, covered with a layer of black dust sticking to their sweat, looked like devils. The tired horses, no longer off-saddled, had large open sores on their backs. The heat was burning, thirst intolerable... We kept advancing without knowing why or where... We knew nothing, and we continued our march as in a dream, under the scorching sun, gnawed by hunger, parched with thirst, and so exhausted by fatigue that I could see my comrades stiffen in the saddle to prevent themselves from falling…

The 4th Dragoon Guards watched three troops of the 9th Lancers charge a Regiment of Uhlans, who overran them. This would have a devastating effect on our story, for Otto's life would now change totally, instantly and forever. But what happened is shrouded in confusion and mystery. The family heard the story, possibly from Otto's comrades who returned from the battle, that his horse was hit by Allied enemy gunfire, and fell on top of him, so that he was held fast by the arm under his horse, and could not escape. According to Berlin central hospital records he had been slightly wounded, not specifying how or when. Regimental records simply describe him as having been wounded and taken prisoner.

Let us put two and two together. According to the Regimental history, they had crossed the Marne. Then the massive counterattack of the British and French armies forced them back over the river, under heavy rifle- and shell-fire. Part of the duties of the Uhlans was to cover the retiring Army, so Otto would have been working feverishly to cover the retreat, standing between the German and the Allied armies. But then the bridges over the Marne had been destroyed by British engineers to hamper the German advance, so Otto would have found himself on the south bank, unable to retire further, facing the advancing Allied enemy. The Allied artillery barrage and infantry fire would have rained down upon him, when his noble horse fell, mortally wounded by Allied enemy gunfire, and rolled on top of him, pinning his arm to the ground. He must have been trying desperately hard to wrest himself free and escape before the advancing lines of Allied enemy troops got there. But now they were on top of him; and he was captured by the French vanguard.

How appalling it must have been for Otto in these circumstances; not even his comrades could have helped him as he was cut off from his Army by a river that he could not cross and the Allied enemy forces, mounting a staggering counter-attack, were all but on top of him under a hail of fire-power. After all the struggle and emotion of recent weeks, he was being abandoned with their goal just over the horizon.

A diary taken from a captured German cavalry officer was handed over to British Staff Headquarters at this time. It gives the most graphic account of what Otto would have gone through that day:

The whole Regiment is destroyed - every horse and every man is lost.

The enemy's columns and artillery are on all sides. After 15 minutes rifle fire we came under such a heavy shrapnel fire that we did not know where we were - we got into a ditch and clawed the ground. I have never spent such an hour.

They were all too exhausted to fight now. The advance had been a massive achievement but no amount of exhilaration and verve could make up for their screaming fatigue. In a letter found on a Regimental cavalry doctor reporting to a divisional doctor shortly after this date, we read:

Through want of food and rest during the last days the men of the Regiment are for the most part so exhausted that during every short halt in the day they fall asleep on horseback and in my opinion are no longer fit to carry out their duties with care and thoroughness.

And in a letter found on another officer:

For 4 days I was under artillery fire - it was like hell only a thousand times worse ... our morale was absolutely broken.

While, on this day, Otto Scholz of the 3rd Uhlans was wounded and taken prisoner, and would be taken to Netley hospital, as the German advance was halted, and fell into retreat. To his family, all trace of him was lost until he died at Netley on the 14th December 1916.

The cavalry of both sides had gone to war, just a month earlier, champing at the bit to uphold the honour and traditions of the *arme blanche* and had learnt - for most of them, too late - the lessons taught a generation before, amidst the struggles in the Franco-Prussian War that had defined the effect which modern technology had on Napoleonic tactics. Both sides now realised that the ferocity of modern firepower forced them to dig in, as the only way to hold their ground. So they started to dig, feverishly, with extraordinary speed, as British and Germans furiously struggled to beat the other in a race to the Channel coast, in order to outflank the enemy's trench and attack him from the front and rear. The British trenches were not really intended to be permanent affairs; they were hastily thrown up, then protected with a tangle of barbed wire. But permanent they became, and the age of technology ushered in a new age of warfare, which rendered the horse in war a useless anachronism.

On the 20th September, the 4th Dragoon Guards turned out at 04.00, but it was 12.30 before they received firm orders, to move to a position of readiness near Paissy. Then there was another, uneasy pause as they took cover from German shell fire, when they received a message that the West Yorkshire Regiment had been heavily attacked and driven back from their hastily-dug trenches, in an effort to break through the British line. The indefatigable Major Bridges led B Squadron to the trenches, where the charges jumped steeplechase-fashion, then led the West Yorkshires to the Chemin-des-Dames, and returned to the trenches in support, until 21.00 when some reinforcing infantry arrived to relieve them. The Brigadier General commanding the 2nd Cavalry Brigade had this to say:

I wish to bring to the notice of the 1ˢᵗ Corps Commander the 4ᵗʰ Dragoon Guards who have consistently fought so well in the campaign and nothing could have been finer than their action today.

It was gallantry in the classic style, but at what cost? Sidney Charles Good was a Private in the 4ᵗʰ Dragoon Guards. He was an Essex man, and lived in Leyton with his wife Edith May. Having started the war in the very vanguard on horseback, but now they found themselves as foot-soldiers with rifle, pick and shovel in the race to the sea. But as the cavalry was feverishly fighting shoulder to shoulder with the infantry to avoid the Germans outflanking them and getting behind them, Sidney was severely wounded, and evacuated to Netley Hospital, where he died on the 2ⁿᵈ October. These trenches had turned it all into a war of static positions with little or no movement, in which the brave and noble horses no longer had a future but for annihilation on the barbed wire and machine guns. In such terrain, even armoured cars could only patrol the roads. But the troopers themselves had been well-trained, and such a large resource could be better employed as infantry, while their mounts could replace the losses sustained by the horse-lines of the field artillery operating in the rear of the trenches.

Meanwhile, the troopers of the 3rd Uhlans were still in the saddle. *Rittmeister* Albrecht von Roeder was leading his men across the Aisne, striking the British in a swansong of the old order of cavalry, firing their rifles as they attacked, before they clashed, sword to sword, fist to fist, at close quarters with the British cavalry. But in a moment they were stopped in their tracks, and found themselves under heavy infantry fire. Perhaps it was this sort of action that encouraged Britain's General Haig, a regular cavalryman who stubbornly held on to the horse in war, to keep his cavalry in readiness, training the men accordingly.

Riding ever further from the field of battle where Otto had fallen, ten days later they were sent to the Eastern Front, where the Russians had trounced the Austro-Hungarian armies. If they were not stopped they would invade German soil and overwhelm the Scholz family heartland in Silesia; Otto would not be with them to defend it.

CAPTIVITY

3rd Uhlans in the trenches.

As a proud Brandenburger, the son of a distinguished German dynasty and an élite officer of Uhlans, Otto Scholz must have suffered a thousand agonies as his enemies caught up with him, knowing that he had no hope of being rescued. We know that he was captured by the French; it is possible that he had been lightly wounded when his horse fell on him, as the family had been told, so he would have been taken to a casualty clearing station, probably at the nearest railway station in Meaux itself, where patients could be evacuated as quickly as possible. Perhaps because the French handed him over to the British as a prisoner of war, the whole picture is unclear and confusing from this point; whether by accident or design, nobody can tell. We know that five German Officers of the Reserve were taken prisoner, but in a month when German casualties totalled a staggering 125,423 it is perhaps not surprising that facts and reports are confused. Whichever way it was, the British and the French had to observe the Geneva Convention and treat the wounded without favour.

At the time when Otto was separated from his Regiment, the whole war was turned upside down, and rôles reversed in a bewildering change of fortunes. For the men of the 3rd Uhlans, as for the rest of the German armies, the next hours and days proved as desperate, as chaotic as the early days of the retreat from Mons had proved for the Allies. Positioned, as they were, on the right flank of the 1st Army, the 3rd Uhlans were completely cut off from communication with the headquarters of High Command, which was burning to hear the news which only they could give: the generals' eyes had been blinded, and they were helpless. Every movement of their sudden, urgent, general retreat seemed endangered and entrapped by the hammer blows of the Allied counter-attack.

Amidst the confusion, every man, from von Linsingen to the most junior trooper, understood that the only way to take some pressure off their Army was to fight back hard and attack; so, in the early hours of darkness, the troops that were gathered on this right flank made an encircling attack against the French northern flank that had hit them. Come first light, German aircraft reconnaissance found the artillery batteries on the French northern flank were slowing their rate of fire and their forces east of Bregy were seen to be standing in formation to move out. But they were not retreating; they were going to advance. The British advanced movement was pushing against the Marne. When the flyers reported back, High Command took the only decision that was feasible, and abandoned the reconnaissance operation to the south. The Uhlans would be needed sorely in a new task now.

The Germans had to withdraw, there was no doubt about that, and the backs of the 1ˢᵗ Army would have to be protected from the Allied push, so it was important to conceal the High Command's intentions from the Allies, and protect the rear with the utmost cunning. Now von Linsingen's men had to reconnoitre in a south-easterly direction, to find out just what the Allied enemy was doing, so *Leutnant* von Stutterheim and Squadron Sergeant-Major Flume set out with their patrols. They did not have long to wait and soon were reporting Pecy fortified by British cavalry, which had gone ahead of their main forces, just as the 3ʳᵈ Uhlans had done on their advance through August. When von Linsingen received the report from the patrols, he sent the rest of the Regiment out, and cleared Pecy of the Allied enemy cavalry. Well, that was what was stated in the Regimental records, anyway - for this was a general rearguard action and, as the cavalry division retreated, the 3ʳᵈ Uhlans had to play a defensive rôle, with von Linsingen in charge of the covering fire on the high road two kilometres north of Pecy, covering the bulk of the division.

But Ensign von Dieze stayed behind in the town with five troopers, to spy out the Allied enemy at close range and, far from having been cleared out of town, the Allied enemy cavalry was there in force. It was a dangerous job for the Uhlans, of course and they were going to have to make their exit pretty rapidly. In fact, they nearly did not make it at all; breaking cover to return to their unit, they were quartered by some of the town's inhabitants. A tense moment followed, then one of the townsfolk said:

Vous êtes Anglais?

Ensign von Dieze nodded, *Oui, oui!* and a patriotic old boy embraced him with heartfelt passion. Then, released from this happy embrace, they continued their withdrawal (or, as the French inhabitants believed, their advance).

It is always unpleasant for soldiers to have to evacuate a place that they had held, such as this, but orders are orders, and they simply had to follow their retreating Army, leaving in a disorderly line, leading their horses on foot. They had left it at the very last possible minute, as well, for the British had overtaken their position with a strong force. It had all seemed a bit too easy, though - and it was, for, as they reached a point about 100 metres from the outskirts of the town, they were fired on with a volley - maybe from British troops who had spied them out, or maybe from the townspeople themselves who, now, had discovered their mistake. Still, they did not suffer any casualties.

The Allies were now treading hard on the heels of the German Army, forcing the Uhlans to swallow the bitter irony of passing towns and villages that they had encountered so recently in their triumphant advance. But it was not, by any means, the headlong flight which had clogged Allied arteries with chaotic scenes of panic and the Germans were selling their ground dearly. Now it was as vital as ever to keep a close eye on what the Allied enemy was doing, and General von der Marwitz learned that a British force was approaching La Ferté sous Jouarre with only some artillery and weak infantry, while their headquarters were marching east, obviously with other priorities on their minds. So he sent the 2nd Cavalry Division with some Jäger support to the heights above Cocherel, to see what was going on. East of La Ferté, the Allied enemy was advancing northwards, across the Marne. Thousands of them.

The horsemen had a bonus, for they succeeded in linking up with the 5th Jäger Division, and they had a bold idea to give the enemy a bloody nose, here and now, when the order to withdraw was received. It was a disappointment to turn away, but theirs not to reason why, as a British poet described a much earlier engagement. Cold comfort, though, to content oneself with the satisfaction that some enemy soldiers would never know how close they came to death, just there.

The 3rd Uhlans moved back to continue covering the retreat: all, that is, except for the 2nd Squadron. They were to stay on the Marne, to report the Allied enemy concentrations. They were to be the last German troops on the river. One patrol rode for La Ferté, the other Ussy to the west, to watch the British at the Marne crossings, on the banks and the bridgeheads. It was something of an anti-climax, though, for there was not much more really to be gained by them being there; they would be more valuable back with the rear-guard, so the Squadron was ordered to re-join the division. The trouble was, those orders had been delayed in reaching them - and by the time they received the instruction to turn back, the territory that divided them from the rest of the division was a very dangerous place indeed.

The Squadron rode back via Cocherel, but the division had long moved out. The country was deserted, in anticipation of the Allies overrunning the position at any time. They only met a few wounded Jägers and some shell-shocked infantry who were quite out of their minds. Some five kilometres northwards, they caught up with a company of the 3rd Jägers and a long baggage column. They thought they might be in Allied enemy-held territory, when, suddenly, a shrapnel shell exploded nearby; obviously the enemy did not share their opinion of the geography. They knew that there was a bridge nearby, which they could cross to continue their journey but, when they reached it, they found it blocked by wagons trying to get across. There was no way in which they could get through, so they decided that they would have to move on, when a barrage of artillery fire suddenly came down on the bridge position. Wagons rushed for cover, while loose horse-teams galloped away and added to the confusion - but the wagon train was moved, at least, and the Uhlans could press on.

With communications completely lost, they had no idea of where they should go to catch up with the division - north, east or west. An artillery duel was being hotly contested from the east and from the west but, which was the enemy's, they did not know. They had to continue their journey, though; so, in the words of the Regimental History, it was *Line-Up; Gallop - March. Some shrapnel shells sang, but they were too high, and too short.*

It was a quite extraordinary experience for them; caught between two massive armies, one their own, the other the enemy's, but here they found themselves utterly alone - one huge, yawning, empty battlefield, the only companionship being the sound of artillery fire coming from somewhere. The spell was broken at Dammard, where they caught up with a long column of ambulances. Then an almighty artillery attack came down, and shrapnel tore apart the wagons. Right in the midst of it, the Uhlans could only get an incomplete picture of the situation, with the gunfire and shell-blasts around them; but they still could not see any sabre troops - no cavalry at all. Their task seemed hopeless.

Then, finally, they spotted some Squadrons at the trot. Incredibly, they had made contact with their own Regiment. As the Regimental history put it, it was a wonderful accident; the chances against it had been enormous but the reunion was tremendous. That night, the Regiment's four Squadrons - or, rather, what was left of them - bivouacked near Soissons, grateful to be alive and with their comrades once more - but they were now well north-east of La Ferté, reversing the triumphant advance they had so recently achieved.

Those desperate German riders were men whom Otto knew well, they were his comrades and brothers in arms and, very possibly, had seen his fate. But that fate was taking him ever further away from his comrades. Having been wounded, he would have arrived at the casualty clearing station, where a doctor would have made a hurried examination of Otto's condition - with the appalling number of casualties coming in, it could not have been anything else but hurried - and his wounds would have been dressed as best as could be done in the nightmare conditions there. What is not clear, however, is precisely what injury he sustained, for those records have been lost without trace in the course of the last hundred years. No doubt such a disappearance is possible, or at least understandable, for documents get destroyed in the course of ninety years, two world wars and a social upheaval. Just once in a while, new documents emerge from deep shadow into the sunlight and reveal a new insight into a mystery that turns an accusation into a defence.

Now that he was in the hands of his enemy, just what sort of interest might the British have taken in a man with Otto's family connections? The evidence of routine intelligence procedures from daily intelligence reports in the National Archives would suggest that they may well have singled him out for special attention, because of his social and professional or diplomatic associations; the Geneva Convention permitted such questioning, provided that he was treated humanely. Such a question certainly arose in early 1915, when the personal effects of an aristocratic officer, *Rittmeister* Freiherr Marschall von Bieberstein, were discovered on the battlefield, and forwarded by Army Headquarters in Havre to London, where the vexed question was considered, of what should be done with them. It was vexed because of the very reason of the late owner's apparent connections. The Foreign Office sent a memorandum from Sir Ralph Paget to Sir Eyre Crowe of the Prisoners of War Information Bureau, on the 25th January 1915:

Do you know anything about this man? I think the usual notification to the German government is quite sufficient especially in view of the fact that the Germans scarcely ever notify to us the names of the British officers they pick up dead etc although we have continually reminded them of this obligation and some 100 British officers are unaccounted for.

William Lawrence of the Bureau, replied:

Among the miscellaneous collection of papers docketed 'Taken from the German dead' and forwarded from the General Headquarters at Havre about the 9th December was the Soldbuch (pay book) of Hauptmann Freiherr Marschall von Bieberstein. I have made enquiries to see if further information could be obtained but the Intelligence Department reports that:

As the fighting was keen at the time, no further investigation was possible. The presumption is that the book was taken from the body of a dead officer. But there is no proof.... It is our practice to report such cases to the German Government with the following note:

"The effects of ------ have been forwarded from the Base with a covering note to the effect that it was not known whether their owner was dead or a prisoner. They have not been traced to a prisoner in the hands of the British Government during the course of searches extending over a considerable period of time, and accordingly the name of the owner is not given in the list of German Dead."

In view, however, of the social position and the diplomatic connections of the deceased officer, Sir Paul Harvey thought that the Foreign Office might possibly have more exact knowledge of the family of the officer in question and might consequently wish that the official notification should be preceded by something in the way of an official communication to the relatives.

The question seems to have been settled by Sir Horace Rumbold who replied on the 3rd February:

The usual notification to the German Government would seem to be quite sufficient.

This tells us that the British authorities continued to notify the Germans of evidence regarding their dead or captured personnel, and that their status would not have affected the situation. But can we reliably draw this conclusion of Otto's position? Why was he handed over to the British by the French in the first place? Why was he then detained by the British, either at Netley or elsewhere, amid passing the information through normal channels to Germany? Such must have been the case, because, firstly, his family, distinguished as it was, learned hardly anything about his condition or his whereabouts; secondly, even the Foreign Office had not been kept informed.

No love was lost between the Allied and the German governments at the time, which otherwise might have assisted. The withdrawal of their respective ambassadors in such a rush had even left their private effects and furniture stranded in enemy territory, and only after much diplomatic to-ing and fro-ing was it settled that, if the British sent the Germans' furniture and effects to the Hague for collection, the Germans would do likewise for the British property languishing in Berlin, Dresden, Munich and Darmstadt. It all took months, partly because, with their respective embassies closed, communication was conducted through the neutral offices of the United States. Meanwhile, the mutual enmity permitted preciously little sympathy for prisoners. In reply to a request from the British Government, Berlin replied via the United States Embassy in Berlin, on the 18th January 1915:

The dispatch of English literature to the English prisoners in Germany cannot be permitted on military grounds. There would be a danger that with the literature, unauthorised information might be conveyed, the spread of which amongst the prisoners would not be in German interests.

Suitable literature will be supplied to the prisoners from here, so far as it may be so required.

Precisely what could have been the conflict of interests between the prisoners and the German powers is difficult to divine, unless it was in German interests to keep morale among British prisoners as low as possible, and the adjective *suitable* when describing the literature which the Germans would distribute, sounds less than refreshing. The next paragraph explains, possibly, the motive for this decision, though, in a tit-for-tat exercise:

In this connection it is pointed out that the French Government have apparently drawn even closer limits; for according to a statement of the French Red Cross which has become known here, even newspapers may not be used to pack parcels for the German prisoners.

We have a rare insight into a prisoner of war camp for German officers in Britain, for a report survives, of a neutral inspection conducted in 1915, of the camp at Donington Hall, near Derby - where a certain *Leutnant* Kurt Nickish had been detained, as we shall see, before he was listed for repatriation. At the time when it was inspected, new huts had been built in the grounds, each of which would accommodate 18 officers, but they were not yet in use, so all 156 of the German officers were installed in the main building. Donington Hall was described as a stately, eighteenth century home set in a splendid park, with cattle, red deer and fallow deer which could be seen in all directions from the front of the building. For us, this report carries great importance, for Otto was transferred here after a *protracted*[33] stay at Netley hospital from his battlefield wounds.

The officers managed themselves with a General Committee, which

---

[33] The word used by the Foreign Office in December 1916 (FO383/287)

comprised the senior officer and three others, and the food committee of three officers. The cost of food was 2/6d (12½ pence) per day for three meals, with an additional 3d for tea. A few of the officers occupied themselves with carpentry, with classes, also, in languages, shipbuilding and science. A music society was also mentioned, although physical exercise was freely available as well, with 10 acres of land fenced off for the prisoners' recreation.

Sleeping accommodation consisted of bedrooms that contained between one and 14 beds, depending on the size of the room. The only one-bed room was occupied by one of the three civilian internees, the very well-connected Friedrich von Bulow. The largest one, with 14 beds, measured 35 feet by 24 feet. There were fires or stoves in each room, and the iron-sprung beds had hair mattresses, sheets and four blankets. A wooden chest of drawers and washstand was shared by each pair of prisoners. In addition to the bedrooms, the officers had sitting rooms on the ground floor, dining rooms and very adequate sanitation. There was also an infirmary, containing four separate rooms with two or four beds, although there were just two cases in the infirmary at that time, one case of slight fever, and the other case was one of nervous strain.

The conditions in which prisoners of war were held, became the subject of much debate in 1915, after the British public heard of the outrage against an unarmed merchant ship, the *Oriole*. Perhaps this was the turning point in history when the human rights of men in war lost their way.

The laws of procedure for naval operations were documented in the Manual of the Laws of Naval War published in 1913[34] which strictly

---

[34] Manual of the Laws of Naval War, Oxford, Adopted by the International Institute of International Law, August 9, 1913; see http://hrlibrary.umn.edu/instree/1913a.htm

forbade pre-emptive destruction of merchant ships and consequent loss of life on board. Under Article 32, any merchant ship may be summoned to stop, when the belligerent vessel would send a boarding party to conduct a search for illegal cargoes of war. The Laws required that, after the belligerent had fired a warning shot, the merchant ship should then respond by signalling and then *stop at once*. The Manual did not give advice on what the warship should do if she did not respond, but Article 17 forbade killing or wounding an enemy who had no means of defence; subsection 2 forbade a belligerent from sinking a ship which had surrendered, before having taken off the crew –but was silent on what to do if she did not surrender. Article 18 emphasized that *it is forbidden to destroy enemy property, except in the cases where such destruction is imperatively required by the necessities of war or authorized by provisions of the present regulations.*

The passenger-cargo ship *Oriole* was owned by the General Steam Navigation Company and registered in London. She was brand new, her paint hardly dry when she sailed from London on Friday, the 29th January 1915, bound for Le Havre with a hold full of general cargo for the war effort. The crew, all Londoners, were experienced seafarers whose ages ranged from 23 to 53[35], and would have been thoroughly competent in the safe manning of this fine little ship, which had a speed of 12 ½ knots, certainly respectable for such a vessel but, by no means, would it have enabled her to out-run a submarine. Up until this point in the war, the Owners had no reason to doubt that the Manual of the Laws of Naval War would be observed. That being said, she would have been in the safe hands of her Master, in whom the Company and the Flag State reposed all their confidence for the safe navigation of the vessel to avoid disaster, if such could reasonably have been avoided.

---

[35] https://greatwarlondon.wordpress.com/2015/01/30/ss-oriole-and-the-blockade-of-the-uk/

The next day, a small British-flag cargo ship, the *London Trader*,[36] passed her off Dungeness; it would prove to be the last sighting of the *Oriole*.

She was due to arrive at Le Havre later on the 30th January, but was reported overdue, and disappeared without trace. On the 6th February, two lifebuoys from the *Oriole* were washed up on the shore at Rye; then, on the 20th March, a bottle was found by a Guernsey fisherman containing a message merely stating:

Oriole torpedoed – sinking[37]

The handwriting was confirmed to be that of the ship's carpenter, 50-year-old Reuben Swain, by his widow, Eliza.

Subsequent investigation drew the certain conclusion that the *Oriole* had been torpedoed and sunk by an enemy submarine, U-20, on the 30th January 1915, 20 miles northwest of Cap d'Antifer. 21 lives were lost, including the Master[38]. Her assailant, Kapitänleutnant Walter Schwieger, confirmed his responsibility in the most damning way possible with attacks on two other vessels on the same day[39].

The British, it must be said, nobly harboured an attitude towards the welfare of prisoners in the early months of the war, but this incident

---

[36] 684 gross tons, owned by Furness Withy of London. The vessel herself foundered just six days later.

[37] http://www.naval-history.net/WW1NavyBritishBVLSMN1501.htm

[38] British merchant shipping losses are recorded in British Vessels Lost at Sea 1914-1918, HMSO, first published 1919

[39] It was Kapitanleutnant Walter Schwieger of U-20, also, who sighted the Cunard liner *Lusitania* through his periscope off the Old Head of Kinsale, four months later, on the 7th May. Ironically, though, that torpedo would have an awesome consequence; of the 1,959 men, women and children on board, 1,198 were killed, including 128 American citizens. In the words of banners subsequently waved by outraged American crowds, Hell was too good for the Hun.

led to a very nasty escalation in the harshness of conditions in which prisoners of war were kept. Following in the wake of the *Oriole* atrocity, the Royal Navy captured the crews of the enemy submarines U-8 and U-12, putting them in detention in Devonport and Chatham. 39 prisoners were taken, some, apparently, wounded, but all, it appears, were put in solitary confinement, as a mark of British outrage of submarine atrocities. The story hit the newspapers with huge publicity, prompting letters to the Foreign Office from the likes of the Brigadier-General commanding the 17th Reserve Infantry Brigade in the UK:

With reference to the correspondence which has appeared in the press, regarding our treatment of the crews of certain German submarines, and the German threat of retaliation - would it not be possible to ascertain through the United States Ambassador at Berlin, whether the German authorities gave orders for submarine crews to behave in this brutal manner?

Whatever the brutality of the German submarine crew for the loss of the *Oriole*, their treatment in captivity raised issues of fairness that demanded some legal interpretation. The Hague Convention with Respect to the Laws and Customs of War on Land had been signed by the UK and Germany and came into force in 1900. Chapter II specifically addressed the fair treatment of prisoners of war. Article 4 stated that prisoners of war were in the power of the hostile government and, that,

They must be humanely treated.

As to any definition of that treatment, the convention appeared singularly vapid and unhelpful; the closest we get is Article 7:

The Government into whose hands prisoners of war have fallen is bound to maintain them. Failing a special agreement between the belligerents

[which there was not], *prisoners of war shall be treated as regards food, quarters, and clothing, on the same footing as the troops of the Government which has captured them.*

At the time of the *Oriole* outrage, the British people had very mixed feelings about the whole issue of the treatment of prisoners of war, but stories of similar atrocities started to unsettle this nation which depended upon the sea for its very survival, and which had not confronted such a despicable threat before. On the 27th April, in the House of Commons, in reply to a question by Mr MacCallum Scott, Mr Winston Churchill, First Lord of the Admiralty, said:

No special considerations are applied to German submarine prisoners because they fight in submarines, but special conditions are applied to prisoners who have been engaged in wantonly killing non-combatants, neutrals, and women on the High Seas. Submarine prisoners taken before the 1st February have been treated as any other prisoners in our hands. But we cannot recognise persons who are systematically employed in the sinking of merchant ships and fishing boats, often without warning, and regardless of the loss of life entailed, as on the same footing as honourable soldiers. Incidents such as the Oriole by night, without warning, with all her crew.... force us for the future to place all German submarine prisoners taken after the 18th February, and for as long as this system of warfare is continued, in a distinct and separate category.

Crucially, for Otto's story, Churchill concluded:

We consider it just and necessary that the prisoners should be separated from honourable prisoners of war who are freed from all reproach.

So what are we to make from this, concerning Otto? Was he, indeed, detained in solitary confinement, which neatly cut him off from prying neutral investigators and German enquiries? Why? He was, surely, one of the honourable soldiers to whom Churchill referred.

Whatever the fallout in Britain, the threatened retaliation in Germany was not slow to follow: 39 British officers were placed in *Arrest Barracks* (a phrase never satisfactorily explained) as a reprisal for the confinement of German submarine crews in the UK. Mr Page of the United States Embassy confirmed the German assurance, that the British officers under arrest in Germany would receive exactly the same treatment in every respect as that meted out to the officers and crews of the German submarines, and that they would be treated as ordinary prisoners of war as soon as the British confirmed that the officers and crews of the submarines held in the UK were so-treated.

Which brings us to the irreconcilable case of James Sanderson. Oswald Sanderson, in an influential position with a substantial Hull-based shipping company to make his voice heard, wrote to Sir Edward Grey on the 21st April 1915, asking after his son James, a lieutenant in the 4th Dragoon Guards (whom we met as the first British Regiment to make contact with the Germans), who had been wounded and taken prisoner, and was rumoured to be one of the 39 British officers now in solitary confinement.

I did not anticipate, barbarous as they are, that they would put a wounded officer in solitary confinement. This is bad enough for a sound mind (they tell me their reason does not last long), but for a wounded one infinitely worse.

Unlike all the previous cases that had come to the attention of the Foreign Office, the case of Lieutenant Sanderson received prompt attention and prompt diplomatic action, by the Foreign Secretary personally. We do not have a copy of his reply but, on the 26th April, Oswald Sanderson wrote again to Sir Edward Grey:

Dear Sir Edward

I am very grateful for your communication of the 24th received this morning, from which I note you have asked the American Ambassador to use his endeavours to obtain my son's release in view of his not being sound. This morning I see in the Press a number of other officers have been taken and some of those also are wounded. It will be hardly fair for my boy to have special treatment over other wounded, nor would he like it, but doubtless the same treatment will be allotted to all. I am deeply grateful to you. I see you have a relation who is wounded amongst them.

Maybe, that last sentence tells us more than the rest of the letter put together. Lieutenant-Colonel Guy Wilson, commanding the East Riding Yeomanry (whose finest hours would come at Dunkirk and D-Day a generation later), and one of the family who owned Sanderson's shipping company, had an awful lot of work on his own plate, as the Regiment was in the course of being transferred to the 1st Mounted Division, in anticipation of a planned move to Salonika but, on the 27th April, he still found time to do the decent thing and write to Sir Edward Grey, thanking him:

Jim Sanderson in fact was very badly wounded in the earliest stages of the war and reported dead to his parents by a private source. In fact he was discovered to be a prisoner of war though wounded by a shell in the back....

A fair picture of British prisoners of war in German hands is not a simple one to grasp[40]; as the months unfolded, gruesome tales filtered back. 30-year-old Private Lee from Liverpool was a Bandsman in the 3rd Battalion Worcestershire Regiment, with the task, as of all bandsmen, of stretcher-bearer in action at the Front. They were among

---

[40] Substantial reports by British prisoners of war are held I the National Archives, see WO 161

the Old Contemptibles who landed in France with the British Expeditionary Force in August 1914, little suspecting the ordeal that they were marching into. When his Battalion retired from Caudry in the intense battles of the 26th August, he was unwounded, but he stayed behind as stretcher-bearer to look after his wounded comrades in a hospital which had been established by the French in the town.

There happened to be an outbreak of scarlet fever in Caudry at the time, so we were put in quarantine and the Germans did not enter the town, but on August 29th a party was sent in to fetch the worst cases amongst the wounded, and these were taken to Cambrai. The minor cases were left in the French hospital, and I remained at Caudry until September 24th. French surgeons were in charge of the hospital, but all patients were British, as well as four stretcher-bearers besides myself.

When the Germans took him prisoner, they were all sent to Doberitz on the 24th September, but Private Lee's experiences here proved to be nightmarish:

I remained at Doberitz until May 1916, and I can corroborate the various accounts which have been given of the bad treatment and privation to which we were all subjected. Life in Doberitz at the beginning was very hard, punishments frequent, and food only just sufficient to keep the prisoners alive. As an instance of the severity of discipline I should like to mention an incident which took place in October 1914 at Doberitz. The prisoners were crowding through a gate, and as one of them, a sailor, who was pushing on in advance of the others, unwittingly reached a part of the camp to which prisoners were forbidden access, he was at once fired at by a sentry and killed on the spot. This seemed to us to be a most unnecessary act, but the lieutenant in command - Baron von Krau was his name - called up the sergeant-majors, and in our presence desired them to inform the prisoners that the sentry would be promoted for having performed his duty, and that on all future occasions such an action would be repeated.

In May 1916 1,000 British prisoners were sent to the Eastern Front by way of a reprisal; 500 went to Libau and 500 to Litau; I was amongst those who were sent to Libau. We travelled from Doberitz to Frankfurt an der Oder by ordinary train, but from Frankfurt to Libau only cattle-trucks were provided to convey us. The journey lasted 3 days and 40 men were packed into each truck. There was only space for half of us to lie down at the same time, and we had to sleep in turns. Two meals a day were given us while we were travelling.

When we reached Libau we had to work at the unloading of ships and received pay, 30 pfennigs per day; the 500 British prisoners were quartered in a large oil store; at first we had to sleep on the floor, but later on bunks were fitted. We were not allowed to smoke, and during the time we were at Libau, as part of the reprisal measures, all parcels were stopped.

In February 1917 we were officially informed that the 500 British prisoners at Libau would be sent to the trenches between Riga and Mitau, and would have to remain within the artillery zone by way of reprisal because the British were employing German prisoners in the firing line on the Western Front.

Shortly after this intimation we were sent off to the Riga-Mitau line; the journey was terribly cold and we travelled in cattle-trucks. On our arrival at Mitau we spent the night in the Russian Lager and the next morning (a Sunday) we started on foot, carrying our blankets and loaded up with everything we possessed in the way of kit, etc.

We had to march 35 kilometres on the ice up the frozen river, the Aa. Seven sledges followed to pick up those who broke down with exhaustion, and the Uhlans drove us on with their lances and with whips. If a prisoner happened to fall out through exhaustion all his belongings were at once seized by the German soldiers whom we passed and who were encamped on each bank of the river; the exhausted prisoner was then thrown on one of the sledges which followed the column, and as soon as he recovered sufficiently he was again put on his feet and made to march on, having been robbed of his kit, etc.

It seemed that suffering best described as Slavery defined the condition in which these able-bodied British prisoners were kept. Private Lee recalled a particularly shocking story while held prisoner at a place called Pinne, in the freezing trenches of the Eastern Front:

I was told by several eye-witnesses of a very gross case of ill-treatment and murder, but unfortunately I cannot remember their names. A party of sick prisoners who had been classed for light duty were ordered to draw carts a distance of 8 kilometres over a road axle deep in mud; this work was suitable only for horses, and on the third trip one of the men, Private Skett (Guards, Grenadiers or Coldstreams?), fell down exhausted, and being unable to rise when ordered to do so, this man was deliberately shot point blank by the sentry and killed. I saw Private Skett's body.

Towards the end of March I was suffering from frost-bite in the hand and general weakness, and after some days the doctor ordered me to be sent to the hospital at Mitau, but it was not until April 13th that I had the chance of leaving Pinne. The thaw had begun, and I travelled up in a transport cart with the two prisoners who had received gunshot wounds when working in the trenches.

The road was so bad that we could only get as far as a place called Kish, where there was a German base hospital. Here we were well-treated, and given the same food as the German patients. The doctors attended to my right hand, which was very badly frost-bitten and most painful. After my 10 days' stay at Kish I felt much better.

We went on to Mitau on April 23rd to the Russian Hospital, which was in charge of German doctors. The patients were attended to by Russian orderlies. My little finger was removed the next day. I was very ill indeed the day after the operation, but they treated me very well and showed great kindness. Parcels reached us here. The condition of my hand did not improve and, as I continued to suffer pain, my right hand was amputated on May 18th. After this operation I made rapid improvement, and they kept me in the hospital until August 1st. Including myself, there were seven British at Mitau Hospital, the two wounded men and four others. We were treated very well and given excellent food. Our letters and parcels came regularly to Mitau.

24 year old Alexander Smith, from Dundee, had worked at a sawmill when called up into the reserves on mobilisation, for he was a Lance Corporal with 13 Field Ambulance of the Army Medical Corps. He had been promoted in the field to Acting Corporal when, in the early days of September 1914, he was badly injured at Dour, near Hainault, being wounded in his right knee by shrapnel from an exploding shell, and suffered a severe kick to his chin from a horse in the ambulance train, which knocked out four teeth. He actually managed to walk to a hospital in Dour where he spent the next three weeks, in the care of an English doctor, and they were left quite undisturbed by the Germans. In October, however, he was fit enough to travel, and was sent far behind German lines, to Sennelager.

At the end of June, in the following year, he was sent to Dulmen, where he acted as an interpreter. But on the 4ᵗʰ May 1916, he was sent to Frankfurt Concentration Camp, where the Germans were assembling some 2,000 prisoners of war to be transported to Russia where they were to be held in reprisal for alleged Allied forced labour of German prisoners behind French lines. He tells the story in his own words:

Four companies were sent to Russia; the one I was in was known as EK1

(Englischer Kommando 1), there were about 600 in it. We started on about the 12th May 1916. I travelled in a second class compartment as I was an interpreter - the men travelled in three boxes which were fitted up for the occasion, and had seats in them. The officer in charge of our company was a gentleman, and saw that we had food equally with the Germans on the train. We got out of the train at a place I do not know the name of, about the 16th May, and had to march 30 kilometres to Kilzeen, where we were billeted in a dirty farmhouse, where we had to lie on straw. We got very little food, the bread supplied by the Germans was all mouldy and not fit to give to the pigs.

I was put in charge of the hospital and looked after the Englishmen who reported sick. There were wooden bunks in the hospital, and we were able to fill our sheets with straw. There were no Germans in the hospital to look after us, as it was no use trying to escape, the hospital being in the middle of a big wood.

A German doctor, Dr Frohlich, was in charge. He kept everything in the hospital clean, and saw that the sanitary arrangements in the hospital were clean. He could speak English, and was a very good friend; I heard that his mother was English. Lieutenant Geise was in command; he was not very good at the beginning but was better afterwards.

The doctor came every morning and afternoon. One morning 200 reported sick; he said they were all shamming - most of them were - and would not look at any of them.

We found a potato pit and so managed to get a good meal of potatoes every day, until our parcels began to arrive.

The men were employed making roads leading to a German aerodrome, and had to work from 6 am to 6 pm, felling and cutting trees. They struck because the work was too hard, the hours too long, and the food not enough. The Germans called in a party of Uhlans with rifles, who had just returned *from the front, and gave the men five minutes to decide whether they would work or whether they would not: some (including all the navy men) agreed to, but others did not. The latter were tied to trees, in some cases being stood on blocks which were kicked away when they were tied up, and left there for one or two hours. Several men came into hospital suffering from the effects. As a result of the strike things improved, as instead of having to having to work 12 hours a day men were put on piece-work; and they were given, say, 10 trees to fell, and when this was done they need not work any more that day. They also began to get their parcels, and having more to eat they were not so dissatisfied.*

The parcels were sent in the first instance from the camps from which we came, where they were censored. In most cases they were half empty when we got them. We were allowed to keep the tins.

We were allowed to write the usual letters and get letters; we were allowed to play football for a time but this was afterwards stopped. I don't know why…

The evidence of such witnesses suggests that the Germans quickly turned to treating unwounded British prisoners with indifference, and then followed a sliding scale to brutality, apparently justifying decisions on the grounds of reprisals for alleged British mistreatment of German prisoners. The care with which the Germans treated British wounded, though, upholds the Prussian Code, and demonstrates a commitment which shines through the fog of war. No better example could be held up, than that of Cuthbert Selby.

When war was declared in August 1914, the Queen's Own Royal West Kent Regiment, part of the 5th Division, was in barracks in Ireland. There seemed to be quite a competitive edge to the business of mobilization in the British Army, and the 5th Division was proud to be able to complete preparations rapidly as it had trained to do, and moved almost immediately to France with the British Expeditionary Force. The men of the original units were amongst the first to see action, at Mons on the 23rd August 1914. 2nd Lieutenant Cuthbert William Prideaux Selby was commissioned into the Queen's Own Royal West Kent Regiment, but transferred to the Royal Flying Corps, where he flew as an observer. He was wounded and captured in the spring of 1916, and takes up the story of his adventures which could form a book themselves:

I was captured at 10 am on the 16th April 1916, being shot down by a Fokker. My pilot was killed by the first bullet fired and the rudder controls of the machine were shot away, so control could not be gained of the machine, which crashed close to Maurepas, on the Somme. I was luckily able to jump clear and landed about 15 yards from the machine.

I lost consciousness just about the time I jumped and regained it about two or three minutes after falling. On coming to, I found three or four Germans bending over me and ascertaining the extent of my injuries. On my asking for water they immediately gave it to me, one of them, as I afterwards ascertained, being a doctor who had come from a battery about 200 yards off.

I cannot speak too highly of the carefulness they took in moving me, going as far as to explain what part of the body they would move next, so as to give me as little pain as possible.

I was then put into a motor-ambulance and my pilot, covered with a rug, was put alongside of me. This ambulance was first taken to Clery, where my pilot ... was taken out and buried. They refused to take me in there, saying they were full up, so I was sent on to Peronne, and taken to an old French hospital there which was then the headquarters of the 121st Field Ambulance, 6th Army Corps.

I was then put on to the operating table and my clothes were quite carefully cut off me, and my most serious injury of the moment was found to be a compound fracture in my left thigh, resulting in partial haemorrhage, and a tourniquet was put on at once. When this was being done, a German orderly hit me violently in the testicles; of this I am quite sure, as I had no pain before, but very considerable for the next few days afterwards.

My other injuries were a broken elbow of the left arm, shin bone broken of the right leg, concussion, and a few other minor injuries.

The events of the next few weeks are naturally very vague, but I will describe what incidents remain in my memory, and these remain very clearly.

I was put at first in a German soldiers' ward, where I was looked after very well; the food was good, but coarse, and in my weak condition I was unable to eat it. The German doctors thought I was going to die, and put up screens around my bed, but on my request they removed them, as I desired to see the daily life in the ward. They also granted my request to receive the Holy Communion, which was given me by a German padre speaking in French.

They also helped me to write a letter; which was forwarded with a full medical report to my people; for I mentioned that my father was a doctor.

Complications and gangrene having set in in my arm, an incision was made. Soon afterwards it was discovered that it would be probably necessary to amputate. They explained this to me and obtained my free consent to perform this operation, if necessary, to save my life. Two more incisions were made, and that being of no avail, my arm was amputated about May 8th.

A very severe bleeding set in about two days later, but owing to the prompt attention of the sisters and nurses my life was saved once more, although they deemed it necessary to bring the doctor in. I stayed in hospital here for seven weeks, the last two being under a different doctor, and my treatment was in every way perfect.

I wish to point out firstly, the absolute devotion and sense of duty of Doctor Haupt, the Oberarzt of this hospital. His whole treatment of me could not have been kinder - always cheerful, always encouraging me and treating me with absolute gentleness in dressing my wounds, which he did about every other day or every day, as occasion demanded it, and in time of excessive pain giving me ether. On his leaving to go to another hospital I thanked him for saving my life; his reply was, "It is nothing; my duty is not to heal Germans, but all the world!"

On the 1st June, Selby was moved by train to a central clearing hospital, where:

The German Flying Corps officers came to visit me in quite large numbers and they were all extremely pleasant and kind to me. I also received visits from the generals of the 6th Army Corps and the 20th Division, both of whom spoke extremely kindly to me and seemed the most meek and gentle of men.

The contrast with the fog surrounding Otto's fate could not be more acute. In the family history, his brother Robert wrote how the family searched for him, trying to be strong but in growing desperation. Meanwhile, the British were still under the obligations of the Geneva Convention to treat him humanely and ensure he received decent medical care. Once those conditions were met, they were entitled to find out what information they could about the enemy from this slightly wounded officer. Article 24 provided:

- Ruses of war and the employment of measures necessary for obtaining information about the enemy and the country are considered permissible.

They even had to pay him. Under Article 17:

- Officers taken prisoners shall receive the same rate of pay as officers of corresponding rank in the country where they are detained, the amount to be ultimately refunded by their own Government.

Unbeknown to the family, though, Otto's condition worsened. He sickened, so they were later told, with a stomach illness that grew ever worse, which somebody attributed to the poor food or the poor conditions in which he had been held. But this much is certain, for it has been preserved in a report by the Foreign Office in Berlin to the neutral American Embassy that was the intermediary for prisoner welfare[41], and dramatizes the whole story of Otto's fate. This document revealed that a German medical officer had been repatriated in exchange with a British counterpart, who informed the authorities in Berlin that Otto's condition was *far from satisfactory as he is suffering a severe disease of the stomach and grave mental trouble.*

The report continued that Otto's condition had grown much worse, according to a communication received from the Red Cross in Geneva, that he had been taken back to Netley Hospital. But from the British, they had heard nothing. It is very apparent that the Foreign Office in Berlin had knowledge of the family, though, and clearly they had been in close communication, because the report referred to:

The serious character of the malady and of the hereditary affliction inherited derived from a mother who has been incurably insane for many years, it seems especially desirable to transfer the officer as soon as possible to Germany so that he may be placed under the requisite treatment in a special sanitorium.

The note had been sent to the United States Embassy on the 29th December 1916; they could not have known that Otto had died 15 days earlier. But by that time, the appalling carnage of the Somme had descended upon and overwhelmed Netley Hospital.

---

[41] FO383/287

THE LIFE AND TIMES OF NETLEY HOSPITAL [42]

We might start our own tour of Netley, with an overview from a book[43] entitled:

REGULATIONS FOR THE GUIDANCE OF OFFICERS AND SURGEONS ON PROBATION ATTENDING THE ARMY MEDICAL SCHOOL AT NETLEY (1898)

The hospital is divided into 2 divisions, medical and surgical.

The Principal Medical Officer has command of all officers and soldiers of the RAMC attached to the hospital, and other officers and soldiers attached to the hospital. and all patients in the hospital ... and will be responsible for the discipline of the whole establishment.

Professors are assisted by medical officers, 2 of whom hold special appointments of Assistants to the Professors of Military Medicine and of Military Surgery. They assist the professors in clinical duties.

The wardmaster of each division attends to the discipline of the patients and of the orderlies, and sees that the latter carry out the instructions of the nurses in the terms of the Regulations.

Nursing sisters: Officers in charge of wards are required to deliver to the nursing sisters their orders with reference to the sick and are expected to give their every support in carrying out the important duties entrusted to them.

---

[42] Primary source interviews of Netley Staff see Sound Archives, Hampshire County Records Office, Hospital records, Royal Victoria Hospital, Netley (92M91/2) and personal papers (92M91/5)

[43] Preserved at the Wellcome Library; e-copy accessed via www.wellcomelibrary.org/item/b18618157#?c=0&m=0&s=0&cv=0&z=-0.7808%2C-0.0805%2C2.5617%2C1.6091

At the turn of the century a visitor, guided by an orderly from the guardhouse, could have seen the hospital at its zenith. The awesome façade of The Royal Victoria Military Hospital at Netley stretched for a quarter of a mile along the shore-line: a gigantic building with an unquestionably Imperial air of dominance, with elegant windows, tall towers and a seemingly-endless, grey slate roof dominated by the Chapel's dome at the centre, soaring heavenwards, and surmounted by a cupola, crowned, finally, with a crucifix. In the grounds, soldiers of the Royal Army Medical Corps trained with the Army Service Corps' ambulance wagons standing by, ready for the stretcher parties with medical officers applying the field dressings. Behind them, the hospital towered over the maturing trees of the landscaped park. Built in red brick faced with Portland stone and plinths of Welsh granite, it consisted of an awesomely imperious-looking central block with two long wings, making a total length of 469 yards, overlooking Southampton Water, with a grand view of the New Forest on the horizon.

Patients were allowed to stroll through the grounds during the day, and along a fine pier, where they could relax in the fresh air; leaning on the railings, looking out over the water, they would smoke their pipes at leisure; we know that, because a couple of years ago the Maritime Archaeology Trust found old pipe bowls on the harbour bed right there. It was a classic Victorian pier, delightfully built of iron that supported the timber platforms, but it had a serious purpose, for shallow-draft ships could moor alongside so that patients could disembark. It was many years later that the pier was finally demolished, but the concrete abutment remains today.

The hospital building was much loved by those people interviewed, such as Arthur Wells:

There were so many corridors there, it took up a lot of space you see, but as regards the building itself, it was a lovely building.

Frank Lawrence remembered the Royal Victoria Hospital from his childhood, for his father was a plumber's mate in the hospital and he would often accompany him on his work. As an old man of eighty, Frank recalled his childhood adventures:

One of the most interesting things was to get into the roof where I can still visualise now, tons of lagging around huge pipes and I can practically smell the same stench from those pipes. I was also shown how to get out onto the roof and unbeknown to Dad I used to get up there on my own and getting up there, the next thing was to get along to the tower, especially on the near side to Netley (village), that tower there for crowsnesting.

There were 138 wards for over a thousand beds, with twelve beds to a ward, designated for medical patients and surgical cases, and officers and other ranks had separate wards. Its design was disastrous though for, as we have seen, it was horrendously ill-suited to serve as a modern hospital. Florence Nightingale had failed to get the plans stopped, and the building never recovered. Amidst the horror of the First World War, when medical facilities were so sorely needed, an Imperial Committee initially proposed to build a South African wing to the Hospital, but rejected it then they realised that, while adequate in summer, the site would not be suitable for South Africans troops in the winter months[44]. They were quite right; the stuffy atmosphere in the wards in summer gave way in winter to numbing cold, for the architect had installed a primitive form of central heating, which really was unsuited to the building. Mr Scott recalled that the radiators were in the corridors anyway, so it was not surprising that the wards were cold and the corridors hot.

---

[44] www.ezitis.myzen.co.uk/southafrican.html

The building itself boasted splendid views alongside Southampton Water that enjoyed the most refreshingly clean air, but none would benefit the wards, which all faced inwards. Mr Scott recalled, the wards never had any sunlight except the two at each end of the building, for the huge windows right along the front face of the building belonged only to the hospital's corridors which stretched from one end to the other on all floors, polished and carpeted and ranked with pot-plants, deck chairs and benches, large window doors, fireplaces, radiators and on the walls, portraits of Prince Albert presented by Queen Victoria. Frank Lawrence remembered those corridors:

The whole length was windows, in the summer months they made that corridor hotter than a greenhouse!

Inside the main doors there was the surprising natural history museum. Or perhaps they understood something of value to the human psyche. Actually, the hospital harboured its own animal sanctuary, albeit an unplanned one. An elderly eye-witness, Mr Pool, recalled:

Underneath the hospital was a long corridor, a tunnel with all the services and everything ... and wild cats. Yes, you gave them a wide berth.

Many soldiers entered the hospital not by the main doors, but by the hospital's own railway platform, connected to the rear of the main block by a covered passageway. As hospital ships grew in size they could only berth in Southampton's main docks, for they were too large to hazard the shallows and come alongside the hospital's own pier. It was then that the railway station became a vital asset. Especially-fitted hospital trains would arrive here direct from the shipside, within a short time of the patients' disembarking.

At the rear of the main block, forming a rectangle, were other buildings that made the hospital totally self-sufficient, with stores, mortuary, bakery, staff canteen and messes, married quarters, gasworks and laundry where the linen was washed after it had been fumigated. One must not forget the sea-water filled swimming pool inside the front entrance off a main corridor. There was even a school for the children of soldiers serving at the hospital; indeed, Annie Johnson had been school mistress there many years, before she died on the 24th November 1913, ten months after her husband Owen, who had been Regimental Sergeant Major of the 2nd Dragoon Guards (The Bays) and both lay buried in the cemetery. Dominating the whole hospital, though, was the Royal Chapel, in the centre, with its magnificent dome surmounted by a cupola.

Alice Coupland recalled:

It seemed a bright sort of place. And every Sunday the people outside if they had passes could go to the hospital church, the wounded all used to go.

Eye-witness Johnny Adams recalled:

It was a lovely chapel. All the patients had to go there Sunday morning … They used to ask you what your religion was, Church of England, or whatever you were. You see you had your own, Catholic was one side, Protestants the other side. A lovely chapel.

Mr Wells remembered the hymns that rang in the Chapel, for the Tommies loved to sing. Afterwards, they would chat with the local people who had come to the service, and many was the time that Tommies were invited home to Sunday luncheon or tea in a local home. Mr Wells commented how well the hospital lived with the local community: *It all seemed to work in so friendly.*

But what about those God-fearing patients who were confined to their beds, and could not get to the Chapel? Mrs MacLean recalled that, after the Chapel service on Sundays, the choir used to go around the wards, and asked what hymns the patients would like them to sing.

The daily routine of a Medical Corps orderly was well-recalled by Mr Potter, a nursing orderly, who got up when reveille was sounded and, in the summer, they had half an hour of physical training exercises or pressed on with preparations for the hospital sports week, carrying chairs or putting tents up. Everybody had their own particular job to do in the wards in the mornings; the fires had to be cleared out and the ashes dumped and coal collected by an orderly, while another prepared to give the patients their breakfast, which had been cooked in the hospital kitchens. After breakfast, the plates had to be collected and washed; then the floors and the lavatories had to be cleaned. Then medicines and drugs had to be drawn from the dispensary and specimens taken to the laboratory for analysis. On one day the windows would be cleaned, while on the next the lockers and the chairs would be. The wooden floors in the corridors were particular features that were remembered, always very highly polished. Wednesdays, Saturdays and Sundays were visiting days, though, so cleaning was not carried out during visiting hours. Of course, there was the matter of lifting and moving patients, and attending to the refuse of a massive, vital hospital. As Mr Smith recalled, the work at the hospital was carried out round the clock, in three shifts, so that patients were cared for twenty-four hours a day.

And the officers?

Very good doctors and surgeons, recalled Mr Smith. *They were very, very good.*

The officers' mess at Netley was a splendid building[45], set apart from the main block, where the physicians and surgeons who cared for the

---

[45] It still is, for it was not demolished with the rest of the Hospital but has been redeveloped into private homes.

patients had their own rooms, and where in high-ceilinged halls they dined and relaxed. It was three storeys tall: on the ground floor were the kitchens, the dining hall, with its anteroom where the officers relaxed, and the ballroom. The first and second floors were devoted to accommodation for some 55 officers. The minutes of the Officers' Mess Committee quite take us back in time; in November 1914, with the pace of work demanding changes in the routine, it was resolved that dinner would have to be changed to 20.00, although in February, March and April it would be put back to 19.30. In 1915, the cost of each meal was increased by sixpence due to the advancement in prices of all food stuffs. While in February 1917, it was decided to have three meatless lunches and three meatless dinners each week, in view of a request just made by the 'food controller'. Mrs Woods recalled that the officers on the medical staff had a ball at the end of sports week and often held dances.

The corridors were served on each floor by lifts that were especially designed to be large enough to take stretcher cases and the trolleys on which the most seriously wounded and, of course, the dead, were taken. All walking patients and all goods had to go by the stairs, though. Mr Scott recalled that the lifts dated back to the eighteen sixties or seventies, and were powered by hydraulics, which must have been a remarkable piece of wizardry for the time, but after a while they developed an annoying habit which could never be shaken off.

They never stopped at the floor level exactly so that if the trolley was brought out it had a six inch drop.

One lift was special, harking back to the very foundation of the Hospital. Queen Victoria had always taken a close personal interest in the welfare of her soldiers. The Hospital's foundation stone, two tons of Welsh granite, had been laid by Queen Victoria on in 1856, when she arrived at the Hospital's new jetty. In May 1900, eight months before she died, Queen Victoria made her last visit to Netley, to see her beloved boys, brought home from the Boer War in South Africa with wounds and sickness. By then she was confined to a bath chair, so the lift that we are talking of was very necessary, as Queen Victoria's own lift; it was very grand, with mahogany panelling, but could only be used by officers or else in emergencies.

Netley Hospital had long been a centre of medical research, and boasted sophisticated laboratories where doctors discovered the vaccine against typhoid and isolated the causes of many tropical diseases that had killed hundreds of soldiers on service throughout the Empire. But even at the turn of the century, experimentation by trial and error was the norm, and a compassionate view to medical care surfaced as a radically modern approach to medicine. Dr Thomas Longmore, Surgeon-General of the Medical Corps, was one of the first and longest serving officers at Netley, and was the world's leading expert on gunshot wounds. He was also Britain's representative at the foundation of the Red Cross in Geneva in 1864. Dr Longmore addressed new surgeons starting their probation there:

I sometimes meet with surgeons who do not seem to consider pain inflicted [by digital pressure on an inflamed eye] as being of any moment. They regard the shrinking from the approaching touch as a mere act of exaggerated sensitiveness or timidity on the part of the patient that does not deserve attention. Might it not be regarded, however, with more justice as an instinctive defence against threatened injury?

As the memory of Empire fades with every passing year, so too does the everyday history that combined to tell the stories of that Empire. How many history books, for instance, reveal that Netley's Imperial business was very much a seasonal one? Mr Scott, late orderly, recalled clearly, though, that in the days of the Empire, Netley saw seasonal work as a transit hospital for patients brought back from all over the Empire at the end of the trooping season. The patients were admitted to Netley from the troop-ships, where they were divided and graded as to whether they were treatable and whether they could still serve, or whether they should be discharged after their treatment. The trooping season took place in the winter and again at the end of the summer, *so for six months of the year Netley would have hardly anybody in it at all.... Then everybody in the Corps had a very easy time, that's when you had the Corps sports and all the rest.*

Seventy years later, elderly, widowed Mrs Woods cast her mind back to those long-past days at Netley and remembered that in the summer time, down at the main hospital building, there were concerts outside on the lawns, and during the hospital's annual sports week, there were all sorts of activities. The staff tug-of-war was particularly memorable; the staff from the asylum block always used to win because they were big, hefty men up there. They had to be, in order to restrain those psychiatric patients who were violent, a danger to others, and a danger to themselves.

By September 1914, nobody had an easy time of it at all. The doctors and the nursing staff had to struggle to close their minds to the tidal wave of horror before them and stem the flow of blood from friend and foe, the care of the wounded always coming first. We must remember that the nurses had day-to-day contact with the people at home; they knew all too well that the people of Netley – indeed, the whole of the Empire – would be relying on them to save their boys. That's the start of it; for you cannot help but wonder how the nurses, many of whom came from local families, who had themselves lost sons and brothers, could have looked upon the German wounded prisoners of war with calm detachment.

When confronted with the fearful waves of wounded, flooding in from Mons, the Somme and Passchendaele, would you or I have resolutely met the medical ethics of a peacetime world? That had been a world which could not have dreamed the nightmare of a frantic struggle, to staunch a stream that never seemed to end, of patients who depended on your skill to save their lives without the technology that made a blood transfusion a life-saving routine procedure; a world which had never given thought to the effect which a million roars of gunfire could have upon a human mind which knew of no escape.

Before the summer was out, the shortage of space at Netley had become so acute that they had to plan a whole new hospital here to double its size, and the Red Cross built a whole new camp of wooden huts behind the main hospital, where Nurse L Ethel Nazer, was waiting to receive the first batch of patients in November 1914. Ironically, these buildings, constructed so hastily from kits and frames, proved to be very much more comfortable and fit for purpose than the wards in the main building, being *light, airy and well-ventilated…. Warmed by slow-combustion stoves… well supplied with water, with admirable sanitary arrangements.*

In these early weeks of the war, Kitchener's call for half a million volunteers was answered with an enthusiasm that was humbling, but it would take two years to train them for the Front. As a result, Territorials were sent out to police the Empire so that Regular Battalions could return home and go straight to the Front. Even then it was not enough, so they had to look to the Empire, and trooped in Gurkhas to the Western Front, to support the beleaguered British Expeditionary Force. With the benefit of hindsight, this was a mistake, for their homeland in the foothills of the Himalayas prepared them for a war in arid mountain heat or dry cold, nothing like the penetrating, wet, freezing conditions of the Western Front, where they suffered far worse agony than the Europeans who had grown up in this climate.

On the Western Front another source of misery was encountered, when the Gurkhas, somewhat shorter than Europeans, took their turn in the trenches dug by British troops, and found them too deep to keep a proper watch on the fire-step, while the trenches which they dug were too shallow for the British troops who relieved them. The Gurkhas were among the first of the wounded to find themselves in the new Red Cross Hospital, the comfortable little town of wooden huts behind the main hospital, where Nurse L Ethel Nazer, was waiting to receive the first batch of patients in November 1914:

Five out of the last twenty were hand and arm wounds and these walked in; the other fifteen were all heavy stretcher cases; some had six or eight wounds from shrapnel and three were badly frost-bitten; one has since died, another developed tetanus and several amputations have had to be done; all the wounds are horribly septic on arrival but it is surprising how quickly they clean up with regular dressing and attention.

The *Evening Despatch* carried a wonderful story in January 1915, where we meet our friend, Nurse L Ethel Nazer again, who had a special place in her heart for a Gurkha who had been blinded but who became the life and soul of her ward:

The other evening, when I came back from tea, I found the patients in roars of laughter. Gundar Singh was out of bed performing a 'pay day' to the other men. I ordered him back to bed, and he immediately stood to attention and saluted. "Saleem Sister Sahib, pay sister Sahib 500 Rupees."

It made splendid reading for the nation at their breakfast tables, but hid the reality that the war was being lost on the operating tables and in the wards in the hospitals, because medical science had not perfected the procedures that enabled blood to be transfused into a body to replace the blood lost in operations to save the wounded. Yet, we cannot ignore that question at the back of our minds, that when confronted with the dignified bravery of those who have come from across the world to fight for us, how far down the list of priorities at Netley would a wounded German prisoner of war fall, with or without the Geneva Convention?

Then there were the broken minds, that filled the asylum with cases that nobody had encountered before: the mental trauma that broke even the bravest men at the Front.

The asylum was known as D Block, built three years after the main complex, and set a quarter of a mile from it, laid out in its own grounds with a pretty little summer house on the lawn, but bounded on all sides by a tall, unscalable brick wall. The very classical, two-storey building looked somehow less grand, less forbidding than the main complex, which yet belied its sad purpose. When the building was renovated in the 1980's, on some of the window panes were found drawings of steamers, surgeons and soldiers scratched in a child-like hand by a forgotten Victorian soldier, amidst his torment served in the service of the Queen. Mrs Woods recalled that patients from D Block…

used to come out on Sunday for a route march. Poor souls, they had neither ties on nor boot laces. There were many wards in D Block, and padded cells. I think it was always full during war time. Shell-shock patients. They had all their own facilities up there because they did not associate with the other people.

The classic beauty of the asylum building was shown off best of all by the grand French windows which opened out on to broad, well-kept lawns, where visitors and staff could stroll in the summer sunshine. This time, Florence Nightingale had had her way and the building was built in the newer pavilion style; but the French windows on the ground floor still only served a long corridor running the length of the building. The building's plan essentially divided it into two parts: the upper storey consisted of an observation area, with large wards, where the patients were rehabilitated, and the sedation ward, remembered witness Mr Potter, was on the left; while, downstairs, the French windows opened onto a corridor. It was not a wide corridor and the most noticeable thing about it was that at regular intervals along its inside wall were thick, steel doors, behind which the most acute cases lived out their lives, and their nightmares, in padded cells. Even the bedding was on the floors, with nothing that a demented brain could use for its self-destruction. At the end was the officers' block, from where you went down a long passage to the new infirmary that was built in 1907. There was a lovely ward there, recalled Mr Potter, as well as padded cells. There were more staff in D Block than in any other part of the hospital, and security was always strictly tight; even the manhole covers were locked, and Mr Pool remembered that *inside D Block it was sunny and cheerful but you had to go through many locked doors.*

Mr Watts said that anybody who had business in D Block was given a master key, so that he could let himself into the different sections, and had to be sure to lock the door behind him. Even so, once in a while, a patient would escape, and commit suicide in the woods outside the high brick walls that enclosed the asylum's own little world. Hardly anything has survived to testify to the life and times of the asylum, for all the records have been lost or destroyed, save a piece of paper, a duty list for the staff on guard duty in the asylum on the 16th May 1916. The day began at 06.00. Under the chief wardmaster, a sergeant major of the Royal Army Medical Corps, guards were posted inside the main building, while another guard of two men were posted in the infirmary. Two, at times three, guards were on duty in the day room, while after 'lights out' at 20.30 twelve guards were on duty.

Theodore Monson was born in Sweden on the 3rd July 1896. His father Isaac took the family to live in Canada and they settled down in White River, Ontario. Theodore was unmarried, a timekeeper by trade, with no military training when he volunteered in Winnipeg on the 3rd November 1915, aged just 19[46]. A fair-haired lad, medium height, he joined the crack 90th Winnipeg Rifles, the 8th Battalion Canadian Expeditionary Force who relished their nickname the Little Black Devils. Having signed up in 1915, Theodore joined the Battalion in the field at the height of the Somme campaign, and would have marched with them towards Passchendaele. Then, he contracted a terrible illness, and was evacuated to Netley Hospital, where he died on the 10th June 1917.

It was not a physical illness, but a psychiatric one, with the most appalling symptoms and consequences. It was called Acute Confusional Insanity, and it was fatal. Theodore would not have presented symptoms for very long, as apparently normal people were admitted to hospital after suffering acute illness within a week, when their appearance and speech were associated with fever and delirium, like a typhoid state[47]. Their decline was rapid, when they would become violent and, when confined to bed, would struggle violently with their nurses. About a quarter of the patients made a complete recovery within two or three weeks, but the rest would die in that time.

Norman Conolly was Medical Superintendent, Richmond (Dublin District) Asylum, and delivered a paper which gives us a clear, but graphic picture, of what Theodore would have suffered:

---

[46] www.bac-lac.gc.ca/eng/discover/military-heritage/first-world-war/personnel-records/Pages/item.aspx?IdNumber=184042

[47] www.bjp.rcpsych.org/content/90/380/761

The disease, when its beginning can be distinctly dated, usually makes its appearance by the occurrence of hallucination. A certain degree of dreamy obscuration of the mind has preceded this stage, as we often find from the statements of recovered patients, but this frequently escapes attention. When the condition is fully developed, consciousness is profoundly engaged. The patient has lost his sense of orientation and his knowledge of his surroundings, or, if he can be roused to correctness on those points, he soon drifts back into the obscure condition. His estimate of time is entirely confused. He dates events of yesterday as having taken place a week ago, of a week ago as being six months old, and so forth. He does not lose his sense of individual personality, or build up an organised system of delusion like the paranoiac....

The duration may be very short, lasting only a few days, or even, in abortive cases, only a few hours... Cases that are about to recover occasionally pass into a state resembling acute mania. Meynert, who first observed this occurrence, thinks that the functional hyperaemia accompanying the maniacal attack brings about a tendency to cure by increasing the circulation of blood through the exhausted brain. More common as an indication of recovery is a slight degree of stupor resembling that through which the patient, convalescing from an attack of acute mania, so generally passes. Prolonged periods of stupor, resembling and probably identical with that occurring in acute dementia, occasionally precede recovery. Less favourable signs are a mixture of maniacal and stuporous conditions, or a tendency towards pathetic and histrionic displays.... As in all cases of acute insanity, death from exhaustion may occur in an early stage, and there is in the usually debilitated sufferers from this disease a special tendency to succumb to intercurrent affections[48].

---

[48] Conolly, N, 1890, Acute Confusional Insanity, Read before the Section of Medicine in the Royal Academy of Medicine in Ireland, on Friday, May 16, 1890, collection King's College London

The first Christmas of the war, in 1914, was a funny sort of time[49]. Mrs Alice Emerson remembered Christmas at Netley:

Christmas down at the hospital was a very exciting time, and they gave the troops all they could to make them happy. And it was decorated all up, paper chains and all that in the wards. Ever so nice. And the tables all laid, spread right out.

It is an extraordinary fact that, for all the evidence of the truce from the soldiers who took part, there is hardly anything to reveal what the people at home made of it when they heard. At Netley, the staff had been confronted with the worst excesses of the war, and the only surviving evidence tells of the festivities in the wards, with highly patriotic flags and bunting to cheer the patients. But, already, a gulf was building between the Tommies at the Front and their families back home, where propaganda was brutalising them against the Germans but they did not or could not grasp the appalling physical and psychological horror of life in the trenches, endured by friend and foe without discrimination. When husbands, sons and sweethearts returned they could not speak of their ordeal, however and the gulf just widened; it grew such, that, in time, soldiers were not fighting for King and Country, or even for their families, but they were fighting for their comrades, and each other. It might be as well to remember that when understanding what this book is all about.

Mrs Woods recalled that the staff put on a show at Christmas, and remembered that *The Mikado* was very popular; but was Otto there among the audience? While slightly wounded, he might have been treated at Netley on arrival to Britain but, after he recovered, he was

---

[49] At the same time, the Christmas truce on the Western Front has been ascribed almost legendary status. For a full account see Brown, M and S Seaton, 1994, Christmas Truce, Pan, London

sent to the prisoner of war camp for officers at Donington Hall, returning to Netley when his condition became acute. Mrs Woods remembered that German prisoners of war were held in Netley, in the main block, but there would have been patients needing high-quality medical treatment: resources were far too precious to permit bed-blockers. While the allied prisoners wore a royal blue uniform, she recalled that the German prisoners had to wear grey uniforms with a red disc on the front and another on the back, which was to be the target for pursuing soldiers if they escaped. A couple did escape, she recalled; they managed to climb onto the buffers of a train which had halted at the hospital's own station, and were only caught at Waterloo station in London.

As you stroll through the military cemetery at Netley today, you will be struck by the number of graves of German prisoners who had died there. They had all been seriously wounded and, in the confusion of battle, were overrun by the British, who rapidly assessed their condition, and took them back to the nearest field hospital, in the same transport as the wounded Tommies. This was no time for a casual exchange of wounded on the battlefield, and the seriously wounded Germans were evacuated to Netley Hospital as prisoners of war, sharing the hospital train with friend and foe alike, for emergency treatment. The medical teams could not treat enemy wounded any less humanely than their own and under the Rules of War, prioritization could not be given to friend or foe, but to the severity of the wound. Article 4 of the Hague Convention 1907 provided:

- Prisoners of war are in the power of the hostile Government, but not of the individuals or corps who capture them.

- They must be humanely treated.

Article 7 went a little further:

- The Government into whose hands prisoners of war have fallen is charged with their maintenance

- In the absence of a special agreement between the belligerents, prisoners of war shall be treated as regards board, lodging, and clothing on the same footing as the troops of the Government who captured them.

Willi Kessler of the crack Prussian Garde Jägers was the first German fatality in Netley, where he died of his wounds on the 18th September 1914; he was 19 years old. Ten days later, Otto Schulz (no relation) of the 4th Garde Jägers died at Netley, while Jägers Eickel, Moikeand and an unidentified Jäger died within five days of each other in October; Jäger Mayer did not even make it to Netley; he died on the hospital ship as she made her way back. Then, in the following month, Privates Grossmann, Hartemann, Niessmann, Heinrich, Stahl and Rehn all died at Netley. The German patients were kept in the wards on the centre floor of the main building, because it had the best security, with floors above and below with armed sentries on guard. It was a bit of good fortune for the Germans (but no more than a bit), that this was the most comfortable part of the hospital, where the whole medical division and B division were taken up by German wounded. But, to do so, the staff *turned our boys out into canvas in the grounds*, as many, like Mrs Woods, recalled.

For all the implied and expressed criticism of such behaviour to *our boys*, this evidence underpins the strong ethics of the doctors at Netley, forming the golden thread running through this story, that they had to fight against the technology that was slaughtering the best blood in Europe. In doing so, they had to struggle to close their minds to the tidal wave of horror they were witnessing being inflicted upon our own troops, but standing up to their sacred oath to stem that flow of blood from friend and foe, as physicians first, last, and always. To them, it mattered not that a German had more comfortable conditions - after all, they had to keep enemy patients securely.

But to the grass-roots citizens beyond the Hospital gates, such ethics were a disgusting betrayal of the fighting Tommies, which brought the Hospital into direct confrontation with the normative ethics of the society that was being brutalised by the war. The men in the shipbuilding yard of Thorneycroft, a short distance away at Woolston, downed tools when they heard of the stark disparity in the conditions in which their own boys were treated as compared with the comfort of the Huns, and marched to the hospital in protest. Other locals joined in the march on the way. When they reached the cricket pitch in the grounds, a deputation was sent to the Colonel Commandant, Sir Warren Crook, who, apparently, promised that they would be moved and Mrs Woods said that a special train came next day to take them away.

Johnny Adams had more special knowledge about this incident. He had been an apprentice at Thorneycroft's shipbuilding yard at Woolston, before he volunteered for the Army. Having been wounded in the arm by shrapnel, he had been taken back to Netley, and was put in the hutted Red Cross Hospital behind the main building. A fellow patient said,

Do you know what they done with us last night?

No, replied Adams.

They took us out of our beds and put us in marquees and put the Germans in our beds.

Put the Germans in?

Yes.

Well that ain't good enough. Look I'll report that to Thorneycrofts.

With that Mr Adams went out and told the whole story to a shop steward at Thorneycroft, when the protest march was hastily organised. In no time at all, the Germans were in the tented camp outside, according to Mr Adams.

So who had the correct version: were the German patients turned out into the tented camp outside because they were on the wrong side, or were they moved to other hospitals by special train, where they could be treated indoors? Or were they not moved at all?

The burial register tells us that spring 1915 had been a busy time for German deaths. The medical team at Netley seemed to be fighting a frustrating battle as the season turned and the death rate got worse. Then there was an abrupt halt to any German deaths. Erich Ruggeberg died on the 11th June and then there were no more German burials for more than a year. Having suffered twelve deaths in the first months of the year, it would be stretching credibility to assert that the sudden drop could be attributed to the case that Netley's survival rate was improving for friend and foe. Yet, there is evidence that there were still prisoners there.

The assertion that they were moved out of the main block is undermined by a newspaper article dated the 6th September 1915, in which the *Nottingham Evening Post* carried a photograph of German prisoners seated quietly at tables said to be at Netley Hospital, guarded by an armed sentry, encaptioned *The men appear to be quite contented with their lot.*

They would appear to be seated in a common room solidly built, which might well be the main building at Netley, and certainly not the timber-built Red Cross Hospital; the windows are not those found at the front of the main block, which would have opened onto corridors, but are the same pattern as those facing east, thus supporting its authenticity. If so, then this says much for the ethics of the doctors at Netley, who stood fast against the conflicting normative ethics of the outside world.

There is further corroboration in another newspaper report that a German prisoner of war patient named Warczak escaped from the Hospital in April 1916. He was recaptured in a wood, two days later, just two miles away, in such a state of collapse that he had to be carried back to the Hospital on a stretcher. He was accommodated at Netley Hospital.

The evidence, therefore, is conflicting. While the newspaper articles suggest that the prisoners were not taken away from Netley, as had been assured to placate the local townsfolk, the negative evidence of the gap in records in the burial register persists, although negative evidence is never satisfactory, as a result of which it is not necessarily indicative that they had been moved.

So let us consider the carnage of 1916. The death toll among the Allied forces at the Somme is told in more detail elsewhere in this book, with gravestones in the cemetery by the score. Four German prisoners, Eirgel (or Erigle), Merkel, Rheinschmidt and Rohwedder, lay buried with the same date of the 11th July, most likely having been wounded in the early days of the Somme offensive, but they had all died at sea aboard a hospital ship and never made it to the Hospital. An unidentified German died at Netley on the 13th July, while Johann Lackmann died on the 11th August, Friedrich Sittig (or Sittit) a month later, Friedrich Molle a month after that and Ernst Plinke on the 18th December. Including Albert Bornschein, a civilian internee who died on the 15th September, that means that six Germans died at Netley in that terrible year of 1916.

It would have been expected to find evidence that the Somme campaign would have swamped the facilities of every war hospital in the country and that Netley would have had to open its doors to prisoners of war again. The evidence suggests that Netley did indeed treat enemy casualties. Given the remarkably high survival rate of the 30,000 patients evacuated from the Somme, a significant number of prisoner of war patients were admitted, which speaks highly of the staff.

Even so, not many tears were shed for the German patients when they were at Netley. VAD nurse Alice Coupland recalled:

Well, I'll tell you straight, I didn't like to look at them or anything because of how our boys was wounded, and of course in those days there was rifles and bayonets and those big heavy field guns that was shooting all the time.

We can understand how the young girl felt. She would have seen the most horrific injuries, and might have met John Nairne. John came from Rosehaugh, in the Scottish Highlands; he had been a keen pupil at the Fortrose Academy, and started an office career blamelessly in the Inverness branch of the Royal Bank of Scotland, where he was said by the local newspaper to have been held in the greatest esteem by his employers and fellow workmen. But the call to arms could not be ignored by such a stout-hearted lad and, accordingly, he joined the Lovat Scouts (then known as Lovat's Scouts), a regiment of commandos fit for heroes. Then, on the 6th July 1917 the Ross-Shire Journal reported that his parents had just been notified that he had been grievously wounded during an advance on the Western Front and, for two days and nights, he lay in a shell-hole before he was rescued. From the casualty clearing station he was evacuated immediately to Netley Hospital – like so many thousands of patients, he would have been back there in a day, wearing the clothes he was wounded in, torn, blood-stained, still caked in mud. His wounds were so severe that the surgeons had to amputate both his legs - one above the knee and one below; while two fingers on the right hand had been blown off, and he had suffered a number of other wounds on the right arm and side. But they saved his life at Netley and, as the newspaper reported, *From all accounts is making a favourable recovery.*

This was a real test of medical skill. When his parents visited him at Netley, they found him bright and cheerful under the circumstances. As the newspaper concluded, *It is sincerely hoped that he may make a speedy recovery, and although maimed, may yet be able for his former work in civil life.*

Friends can become enemies, and you would never have expected it. Many Berlin names are endorsed in Netley's visitors' book in the years before the First World War, a sign indeed of the German Army's medical professionalism, keen to learn from the greatest military hospital in the world. In those far-off days of the late Victorian era, a new German Empire, united behind the banner of Prussia, understood the need for a revolution in medical care, especially in the wake of the Franco-Prussian War, the conflict which baptised the Red Cross. On the 11th August 1873, Dr Hertel, a military surgeon from Berlin, visited, just two years after the end of the Franco-Prussian War, and many more would follow, before Dr Scheike visited from Berlin in August 1891, at a time when Britain's relations with Germany were much more cordial than they were France, who were still seething with indignation at Britain's successful Egyptian campaign in 1882; and very much more cordial than they were with Russia, who were still threatening Britain's Northwest Frontier of Empire, as they had for much of the nineteenth century.

Within a generation, Germans would be coming back to Netley, but in a very different way indeed. Friend or foe, Netley's doctors and surgeons had to battle against the tidal wave of wounded that was now flowing into the Hospital from the Western Front. But, among the men maimed by gunshot and shrapnel, they were encountering something new: casualties were coming in, injured not by physical harm, but by the roar and the carnage of the constant artillery barrages, which inflicted appalling mental injuries on the troops at the Front.

Charles Myers of Netley Hospital had first coined the phrase *Shell-shock*, which he believed to be caused by the physical shock to the nervous system inflicted by the ferocity of modern shell fire. It is a fact that, after the first six months of the war, 15 per cent of the British Army was said to be suffering from shell-shock. Myers' diagnosis would change, when he realised that soldiers' unconscious minds, so distressed by the constant shelling and by the horrors they experienced all around them, crippled their bodies, and effectively disabled them from fighting. In August 1918 Major Hurst and Captain Symns of the Royal Army Medical Corps wrote in *The Lancet*[50]:

From the earliest days of the war we realised that recent cases could generally be cured quickly and completely by a variety of methods, including simple persuasion and re-education, suggestion with the aid of electricity in the walking state and suggestion under hypnosis or light anaesthesia.....Our more recent experience has shown that the prolonged re-education which we had thought was required to convert into a cure the great improvement which followed the active treatment of long-standing cases directly after admission is unnecessary, and we are now disappointed

---

[50] Hurst and Symns, 1918, Hysterical Symptoms in Soldiers, The Lancet

if complete recovery does not occur within 24 hours of commencing treatment, even in cases which have been in other hospitals for over a year.

The assurance of such rapid recovery seems incredible; that being said, corroborative evidence has been hard to find. The key point is that, in these pioneering days, it was all a case of trial and error. In fact, an awful lot of experimentation was carried out at Netley. Mrs Woods recalled the 'scrap shop', a building quite separate from the main block, where animals were taken, *to test them on different things in the pathological room.* It must be remembered, that the surgeons at Netley had their own war to contend with: this war of high-technology killing was bringing critically-wounded men daily, by the train-load. They were watching patients die before them, through simple loss of blood, septicaemia, infection.

Another eye-witness, a VAD[51] nurse who wished not to be named, recalled that anaesthetics were the subject of experiments. Anaesthesia was a young but dangerous science, which required delicacy to render the patient unconscious, care to keep him alive, and equal care to bring him round again. The witness recalled that live animals were an important part of the development process; they would be injected with the anaesthetic, and if they came round, then it was a safe bet that the patient would come round, too. Let us remember that Majors Birt and Leishman had written their paper on pioneering treatment of tropical diseases in 1900 entitled *A New Acid Fast Streptothrix, Pathogenic To Man And Animals.* The biggest killer of British soldiers on Imperial service was not the bullet but tropical disease. In an era when medical breakthroughs were in their infancy, the Hospital would have relied heavily on experimentation.

---

[51] Voluntary Aid Detachment

The animals were kept in a laboratory, where they were looked after with care and, reportedly, much love. But the experiments carried out on them, must have been distressing. The witness recalled an example, when a blood serum was injected to see what results they would get when the animal was brought back from the slaughter house. The result was clear when the blood was found to be full of microbes. The witness recalled with horror, seventy years on, when a human leg was brought into the laboratory, full of gangrene, for testing.

The asylum became the fulcrum of research into shell-shock. Experimentation went hand in hand with observation, and J H Critchley recalled that there was *a machine in there for testing the brain*. He did not elaborate. We know that electric shock therapy was commonplace, as well as a particularly rough form of treatment, shaking the head, which was euphemistically referred to as *massage*.

They made incredible advances at Netley during the First World War, and were justly proud of the fact that just one in eighteen of all patients coming through their doors, would die while in their care. But the awful truth is that they were making those advances in spite of the reckless blundering of the military leaders: not just the British, but those of all the protagonists. It is a remarkable fact, that the First World War had been rehearsed before: in the American Civil War, appalling carnage was inflicted by the use of modern technology in a Napoleonic mind-set. They had rifles, prototype machine guns, and high-powered artillery. At the Battle of Shiloh, nearly 24,000 casualties were suffered out of a total combat strength of 103,000. They even saw trench warfare on a large scale. The Prussian General von Moltke grandly dismissed the war as having no bearing on modern European warfare: then within a decade at the Battle of Gravelotte-St Privat in the Franco-Prussian War, he sent in the Prussian Guard Corps in mass formation - and lost eight thousand men in twenty minutes. Even then, nobody seemed to learn the lesson. The carnage of the Western Front was inflicted because troops were sent Over the Top in the same mass formations, to die on the machine guns and barbed wire.

Of all Man's ingenuity in designing new weapons of mass destruction, surely the most pernicious are brought together in the description chemical warfare. Gas victims were some of the most shocking for the young nurses at Netley. Alice Coupland, whom we have met, was a local girl who had volunteered for the nursing service *because of the other village girls in my village was in uniform, and therefore I liked to do the same.*

She was hardly more than a child when she started her job operating one of the hydraulic lifts, which had been especially designed large enough to take stretcher cases and the trolleys on which the most seriously wounded were taken. She remembered vividly:

Well they (gas attack victims) all had raw red skin and with a lot of them you could only see the two eyes but I don't suppose they could see, because they were blind. To make room, they soon sent them to St Dunstan's Hospital. Other patients had their arms in slings and some were hopping along, you know, where they were wounded in the leg. But the most terrible sights came in as stretcher cases.

Today, as you stroll along the elegant, tree-lined boulevard overlooking Southampton Water and watch the luxury liners on their way to and from the Docks, it is hard to believe that, just one hundred years ago, this was a scene of desperate activity to save the lives of men, wounded, maimed, dying, who were pouring in from the Somme – by the end of the battle, the British Army alone suffered 420,000 casualties. Netley just had to respond to the stagnation of the war that had led to merciless pounding by howitzer and machine gun fire. Every time that an assault was made to break out of the stalemate, the men were mown down by the deadly rain of lead and iron. Eyewitness Johnny Adams was twenty years old when he joined the Hampshire Regiment. He was a Netley boy; before joining up he used to go to the Hospital, where he sold wood at £2 10 shillings a ton to the Gurkha patients there, who had a solemn service to perform:

I used to burn their dead on a big stack of wood in the meadow near the hospital, see. I used to stack this wood up and put the corpses on top, and I'd dance round it!

A brook runs nearby into which the ashes fell, where, according to the Hindus' belief, the ashes would eventually follow the current that would take them into the sacred Ganges. Now, in 1916, Johnny decided to join the Army and go to war himself.

Oh yes, I volunteered. It was a big mistake, though, when I did volunteer. I didn't know what I was going to do, did I? I did afterwards, though.

Johnny had seen some pretty dreadful sights at Netley, where he had visited as a boy, which may have guided him in volunteering, for in that way he had the opportunity to choose what branch to specialise in and he decided to train as a machine gunner in the Hampshires, a 'daisy mower', as he put it, in the trenches where he was sent, but also the target of every enemy gun during an assault. He recalled his job:

Our bullets was only an inch and a half apart going up the barrel. If you put a tin hat in the air and fired at it, you'd keep it up in the air until there was nothing left of it and it would fall to the ground.

Johnny recalled the view behind the machine gun sight:

As you get 'em, if you had your gun and you go like this, 'Brrrrr' they just simply go down like, you know, one after the other and you fall behind one another and follow the man in front. We would mow them down you see.

Then another lot come behind and go down on top of one another.

It was a grim business; Johnny was wounded twice. He recalled with graphic horror, the second time, when he was hit by shrapnel from a howitzer shell:

You see all lumps of iron are blown to pieces, then when that hits you it's red hot. And it's all bubbling, your arm is all bubbling, with blood you see, and Phew, the pain is terrific, you've got a job to stick it.

What stories of pain and suffering lay beneath the graves at Netley, that have simply passed beyond our reach forever? John Arthur Geoffrey Vowler was a Cornish lad[52], the son of Francis Simcoe Vowler and Ellen Frances Anne Vowler, whose fine, white stone home at Edymead House, commanding a fine view of England's summer lands on a hillside in Launceston, would later become the home of the Royal British Legion.

Following the end of his studies at Sherborne, John entered Sandhurst in January 1915, passing out in just five months, when he obtained his commission in the Leinster Regiment. His brother Darrell had been commissioned into the Sherwood Foresters, and was attached to the Machine Gun Corps, where he commanded 179 Machine Gun Company. Whether by accident or design, John also was attached to the Machine Gun Corps where he would learn the skills supporting the Leinsters in the 24th Division on the Western Front, in which a Battalion of Sherwood Foresters volunteers also served.

In April 1916, however, his situation changed entirely when he was wounded in the head while cleaning his revolver, and was evacuated to England. To many, this might be suspected as a euphemism for

---

[52] www.launcestonthen.co.uk/launcestonsfallenfromworldwarone.html

attempted suicide. There were many reports of self-inflicted wounds throughout the war, conduct which amounted to a very serious military offence; in reality, though, it may have been simply accidental – very negligent, but accidental. Investigations were often inconclusive but, nevertheless, placed the soldiers concerned under suspicion. John's case was unusual in that a head wound from a revolver generally was fatal, so, despite the routine precautions in place to guard against accidentally firing a live round from a weapon while cleaning it, the casualty might not have been an attempted suicide. In any event, officers were desperately needed at the Front and John made a good recovery to join the Machine Gun Corps, when he was stationed at Grantham before proceeding to France again in May 1917.

But all was not well with John's recovery and, in July, he was sent to hospital at Rouen suffering from debility, which was defined as a weakness of the patient's body[53], especially brought on by illness. Even at this embryonic stage in the history of psychiatry, debility was associated with mental illness arising out of injury, or out of exposure to the sustained environment of shelling in the trenches. In 1917 it was earning a place under the heading of shell-shock, presenting a whole range of medical conditions described as weakness, fatigue and debility, which were manifestly encountered in hospitals. In defence of the psychiatrists at Netley in 1917, they were doing their best, leading from the front of medical science and, in truth, much of this is still not understood today, resulting in a broad term of War Syndrome, described as *medically unexplained*[54].

By the time that John Vowler had become a casualty, the psychiatric

---

[53] Miller-Keane Encyclopedia and Dictionary of Medicine, Nursing, and Allied Health

[54] Jones, Prof E and Prof S Wessely, War Syndromes: The Impact of Culture on Medically Unexplained Symptoms, Med Hist 2005 Jan 1; 49(1): 55–78

staff at Netley had already started to unravel the tangled web of mental health that was having unexpected consequences for the casualty lists. Shaw shines a particularly useful light in terms of how the soldiers coped with life in the trenches[55]. The medical authorities noticed how the rise in reports of trench foot, winning a ticket to Blighty, followed a comparative trend in the decline of morale among the troops – in other words, as morale declined, the number of trench foot cases increased. In other cases, the High Command took note of a general lassitude, consistent with debility, and lack of aggression in combat – their response was to deplore this as 'shirking'.

The doctors noted another worrying trend, in the number of psychological breakdowns in soldiers who had returned to the Front. This worryingly raises alarm bells with the case of John Vowler. But the doctors had no response to the stress of war, and developed a sort of default position which condemned psychiatric conditions as cowardice.

Jones and Wessely place much emphasis on the relevance of contemporary culture in terms of patterns of thought and behaviour characteristic of a given population, and medical science will be subject to its effect as anybody else would be. Perhaps most chillingly of all, they make the point that the influence of contemporary culture upon doctors and surgeons is most likely to have its most persuasive effect when experimentation and investigation have failed to find an answer; culture gives them the default solution. Jones and Wessely hypothesize that the psychiatric conditions associated with war syndromes were influenced *by the evolving nature of combat: not least the effect of new technology on weaponry...*[56].

---

[55] Shaw, M, How did soldiers cope with war? On-line source of the British Library, see www.bl.uk/world-war-one/articles/how-did-soldiers-cope-with-war

[56] Jones and Wessely, Op cit

We have seen, all too clearly, how Netley had to confront head-on the appalling effects which modern technology had on physical catastrophic injuries, which was also giving rise to these war syndromes, but psychiatry was all but unknown as a science and the soldiers who suffered, were presenting symptoms in different ways, and they simply had to cope in different ways. Today it is called War Syndrome; at Netley they coined the phrase War Neuroses.

For John, it was diagnosed as a serious deterioration in the condition of his old head wound, and he was sent home to England in an extremely dangerous condition. He died at Netley Hospital on the 19th July 1917 as the result of the bursting of an abscess on the brain; heaven knows what appalling pain that must have caused him, which would have spread throughout his body as the abscess ruptured into the ventricular space; today it is often fatal; it 1917 it must have been a certainty. John's body lies in a sadly neglected grave, shaded by a tree that seems to be shrouding it from the outside world.

BEAUMONT HAMEL –
THE FIRST DAY ON THE SOMME

How could the medical teams at Netley possibly cope with the tidal wave of casualties from the Somme? We have seen the evidence that the Hospital had already been struggling to respond to the need to make medical advances in the light of this new brand of warfare. Pushing back the frontiers meant that they relied on experimentation, for which Netley had become famous. Its work developing the science of blood transfusions and of anaesthesia was now stretched to the limit, to try somehow to stand up to the butcher's bill paid on the first day alone, which remains the most disastrous day in British military history. Now we need to put this in the perspective of Netley Hospital; maybe the best way is to look at just one of the battles, and its legacy in the war graves in the cemetery.

There should be a law which demands that history books should only be written by authors who have actually visited the battlefields they are discussing - because it is essential to experience the very geography of a place, in order to understand what took place, and what went through the minds of the men you are writing about.

When you read books about the Somme, you can only hope to imagine the landscape which lay beyond the trenches, where the Tommies went over the top, each confronted with their own square yard of ground to cover before them, in an almost claustrophobic environment, like being in a cauldron. At least in a cauldron, you had an idea of close protection.

When you visit the battlefields of the Somme, the first thing which strikes you is the very expanse of the landscape. It is wide open: mile after mile of broad fields rising up to a ridge, studded here and there with copses and woods, but mostly stands of ripening corn under a very, very wide sky. What is extraordinary, is that the landscape today is almost exactly as it was in 1916; the sector had previously been quiet, and had not been subjected to the heavy fighting and the artillery barrages for which it would later become famous.

As you walk from the British line at Beaumont Hamel towards the ridge where the Germans were dug in, the very expanse puts your understanding in a whole new perspective for, all of a sudden, you feel vulnerable, naked and very, very small, with nowhere to run, nowhere to hide, from the hail of machine gun fire. All of a sudden, you wonder, just whether your artillery barrage might have been effective, as you head out of the trenches towards the enemy – when, suddenly, a Battalion of a thousand men could feel naked and exposed as they advanced in parade ground order, with no cover in this broad sea of open fields.

Before dawn on the 1st July, breakfast was eaten, the kit was packed and Company guides led the men into the front trenches, their steps accompanied by the tympani of their full marching order – a stupid order, for a lot of the kit was not only unnecessary, but by weighing them down and hampering movement it was positively dangerous. The warm sun rose on that summer Saturday when, at 07.20, the mine placed beneath the German redoubt at Beaumont Hamel was exploded. Now would be the time for the whole British front to go over the top and, as the Germans were still reeling from the explosion, the Tommies would clear No Man's Land and take them by surprise – with such incredible force they could not recover from the shock to mount a defence. The Germans would not stand a chance.

But the British did not move. However mystified they were by the inaction, the Germans rushed out from their deep bunkers to man the trenches, strengthen their defences and prepare their machine guns to target the enemy advance that they knew would now be coming.

In fact, the delay was the result of a compromise over incompetent indecision, as to how long they should wait after the mine was exploded. 10 minutes was the agreed delay, and at 07.30, officers blew their whistles along the entire British front, and half a million men went over the top.

As the first wave of Allied troops left their trenches, they were startled to be faced with a devastating barrage of enemy artillery and machine gun fire. It was far stronger than anyone had anticipated. Most men were killed or wounded in minutes. Stanley Whitehead, from Openshaw, Manchester, had enlisted in the 1st Battalion Border Regiment, which had arrived in France in March from Egypt, where they had been evacuated after the monstrous affair at Gallipoli, and went straight into the Western Front in March 1916. He never had a chance. He was seriously wounded and evacuated to Netley, where he died on the 7th July, and is buried in the cemetery. Harry Owen, who had left his home in Chorlton-On-Medlock to join Stanley in the 1st Battalion, died at Netley on the 19th July.

A second wave of troops left their trenches soon after Stanley and Harry in the first wave and met with the same fate. It was now very clear that the artillery barrage that the British had maintained against the German lines for the past week had not weakened the enemy defences anything like the High Command had assumed; indeed, if anything at all, it had created a level landscape of No Man's Land which denied the British any shelter against the German firepower.

The 29th Division had been in the rear position of the Somme since the end of March 1916. Then, in preparation for the battle, they were deployed to the area north of the Ancre River, near to the German-held village of Beaumont Hamel. The Division comprised Regiments whose names resonated a Roll of Honour - the 1st Battalion Lancashire Fusiliers and 1st Battalion Royal Dublin Fusiliers fought in the 86th Brigade, the 1st Battalion the Border Regiment and the 1st Battalion Royal Inniskilling Fusiliers in the 87th Brigade, while the heroic Royal Newfoundland Regiment was in the 88th Brigade. One of the first Regiments to go over the top were the Lancashire Fusiliers[57]. They had been told two days previously that:

To you has been set the most difficult task-that of breaking the hardest part of the enemy's shell.[58]

Unlike the incompetent predictions made to other units, they knew, at least, that this would not be a cake-walk. Between the Fusiliers and their objective lay a sunken road which was chosen as the forming up point, from where they would attack following a huge artillery barrage and a massive mine being detonated at the Hawthorn Redoubt.

It turned out to be Hell. Facing the Lancashires was the 1st Grenadier Regiment from Württemberg, listed as Nr 119 in the Imperial German Army. It had earned itself a tough and distinguished history since its foundation in 1673 and the boys from Stuttgart meant to keep it that way. They had trained specialist sections who excelled as rapid reaction forces, and the ten minutes' grace between the mine explosion and the start of the advance had given them plenty of time to get ready. From deep within their underground bunkers, they rushed up the ladders to prepare for the attack that was obviously coming, and they had the

---

[57] www.lancs-fusiliers.co.uk
[58] Divisional Commander Major General H de B de Lisle

range perfectly. They could see the Tommies emerging from their trenches, and advancing in parade-ground fashion, at a walking pace, their fixed bayonets glittering in the morning sunlight. Many of the British soldiers were seen to be carrying pioneering equipment, to bridge and cross the German trenches they were so confident in taking. Their Regimental history described how the 10th and 11th Companies:

greeted the English with a withering hail of machine gun and rifle fire, effectively stalling the attack. In the section of 9th Company, which had been taken out of action by the mine, brave English bomb-throwers and machine gunners managed to break into our trenches towards the left of the huge crater[59].

The Regimental history saw it as a life-or-death struggle to repel the British attack; no doubt, that was how the Germans felt, desperately trying to survive such an onslaught, and in that first battle they lost 101 dead, including 8 officers, and 191 wounded. But to the British, it was a story of disaster. The Lancashires were scythed down as they struggled to get even as far as No Man's Land, and they did not even come close to meeting their objectives at the German lines. But the British artillery was not making any allowances: they stuck to the predetermined plan and, assuming that the Lancashires were advancing as planned, they moved their range forward, beyond the front German line to the second and third trenches. Nobody told them to pound the German front line again, which could have given some support to the Tommies. As a result, the Lancashires had to fall back to whatever shelter they could find, which was the sunken lane where they had formed up. But then, as soon as anybody showed their head above the edge of the sunken lane, they got mowed down.

---

[59] Gerster, M, 1920, Das Württembergische Reserve-Infanterie-Regiment, Nr. 119 im Weltkrieg, 1914-1918, C. Belsersche Verlagsbuchhandlung, Stuttgart

The Battalion lost 7 officers killed and 14 wounded, 156 other ranks killed and 298 wounded, with 11 missing presumed dead. The 4 Military Crosses and 8 Military Medals that were awarded to the Battalion in that one day were bitter rewards for their part in the worst day in British military history.

But it was not for a coloured ribbon that they were fighting. It was not even for King and Country any more. In 1914 half a million men answered Kitchener's call that *Your Country Needs You*, while the Germans fought *For God, Kaiser and Fatherland*. Now, the soldier on the Front had forgotten the call of patriotism, and was fighting for his mates, as much as for his family - often more than for his family, from whom he was feeling increasingly isolated in their protective little bubbles of propaganda back home.

Another phenomenon was taking place, in the German lines and in the prisoner of war camps, as the unity of so many different peoples started to crumble. The Prussians were increasingly resented by the men from other German States for getting them all into this appalling mess. In a way they were right, for the Prussian *Kultur* was really the dominant force in German government and administration, and the reputation of the Prussian officer went before him, being more nationalistic and conservative than other Germans. A Prussian prisoner of war in England would have been despised by his colleagues from other regions. To them, the recognition of gallantry with its Iron Cross had faded a long time ago. Otto's imprisonment was characterised by resentment and loathing from friend and foe alike. The psychological toll on anybody would have been crushing.

War tends to have its ironies. The Lancashires fighting at Beaumont Hammel were thrown back by the 119th Grenadiers from Württemberg, and were evacuated to Netley, where some would die.

Here the Lancashires were joined by the 119th – for volunteer Max Buggle had been wounded and taken prisoner by the British, then evacuated to Netley, where he had died on the 2nd February 1915. His body lays in the cemetery.

The story of the Somme is a crucial one for us, because it explains the background to the battle which Netley had to confront, to do something for the countless wounded, friend and foe, suffering from the most fearful physical and mental wounds, in a torrent of which there seemed to be no end. Amidst all this, where was Otto Scholz?

THE FATE OF OTTO SCHOLZ

Otto's family never did cease their search for Otto, and the Foreign Office in Berlin continued to communicate with the United States Embassy in Berlin, when it was confirmed as late as November 1916 that Otto was at Netley[60] and, on the 29th December, Berlin proposed an officer exchange for Otto's repatriation.

But it was too late. On the 18th January 1917, the Berlin Foreign office wrote to the American Embassy in a note verbale that it had received a communication from the Red Cross in Geneva that Otto had died on the 14th December:

The cause of the death is given as 'General exhaustion and weakness'. Further details are unknown.

Otto's father had been informed, and accordingly asked the Foreign office to make further enquiries, as a result of which they asked the Embassy for help

With a view to obtaining from the Royal Victoria Hospital at Netley an account as exact as possible of Lieutenant Scholz' illness, his last hours the manner of his interment and his burial-place.

For much of the twentieth century, insanity was a shameful blot on a family, and, so, it is very likely that the family merely passed the story down that Otto had died as a result of a stomach illness. So, no doubt, they continued to believe this when, in the summer of 1987 some descendants of Otto's family visited the grave. It must have been a sad day for them, and they left without discovering the greatest sadness of

---

[60] FO383/287

all, for only since their visit has the Author carried out this research and traced the death certificate.

Frederick Clendenning was a Member of the Royal College of Surgeons (not Physicians, incidentally, as one might have expected in the case of a psychiatric patient). He was not a regular officer but was in a senior position at Netley for he was in personal attendance on Otto in the closing days of his life. While the Red Cross had been informed that the cause of death had been exhaustion, it was now certified that the immediate cause of death was:

Mania (acute)

A secondary condition, contributing to the death but not the immediate cause was:

Exhaustion.

By now, everybody had forgotten about the report that he had been pinned down under his horse by his arm. No doubt, therefore, that Otto had recovered from any associated injury in his first stay at Netley.

Nevertheless, a medically trained barrister has advised that, as causes of death, these would be unacceptable today and even in 1916 may well been unsatisfactory. So let us look at the causes of death more closely:

1. Acute mania described a form of insanity marked by great emotional excitement, by hallucinations, delusions, physical excitement and a tendency to violence. It could have followed acute depression after Otto's capture and long imprisonment - psychiatry was unknown in 1916; but even then, could not have been considered a cause of death: nobody has ever died of madness. Of the medical case records in the Public Records Office not a single one refers to acute mania, but we do have evidence that acute mania had been recorded as a cause of death

in other patients at Netley. Moreover, the association with Otto's mother who had apparently suffered serious mental illness must have been a key factor in the psychiatrists' diagnosis of Otto's condition.

2. Exhaustion described a loss of vital and nervous power from fatigue or protracted disease, perhaps resulting from the physical excitement symptomatic of acute mania.

In 1933 Derby analysed mortality in patients with manic depression who had been admitted to Brooklyn State Hospital and discovered that, between 1912 and 1932, 980 of the patients died during their stay[61]. In 40 per cent of those cases, the cause of death was determined to be *exhaustion from acute mental illness*. Sometimes, however, exhaustion was used to describe the effect of loss of blood or haemorrhaging. But loss of blood would be a very suspicious symptom to find in a man who had been a patient, or at least a prisoner of war, for more than two years.

While there is no evidence of other medical practitioners certifying such causes, Clendenning did certify this cause of death in another patient, a British soldier. Corporal A Brooks of the Royal Engineers died a month before Otto, on the 14th November 1916, aged 38. Clendenning was the certifying practitioner when he reported the death as being due to:

Mania (acute)

The contributing factor was stated as:

Cardiac failure.

---

[61] Derby, I, Manic-depressive "exhaustion" deaths: An analysis of "exhaustion" case histories. Psychiatric Quarterly, 1933;7:436–49.

In July of the following year, Theodore Monson died in D Block with the cause of death determined to be Acute Confusional Insanity. So we can conclude that there are other cases which validate the sincerity of the defined cause of death, and the suspicion of any professional misconduct therefore diminishes into remoteness.

But how can the manic-related cause of death be reconciled with the cause reported to the Red Cross of *General exhaustion and weakness*? And how can either be reconciled with the cause of a stomach illness? The apparent inconsistencies are bewildering, and medical authorities should be professionally beyond reproach which arouses suspicion because of the inconsistencies.

All that being said, we know that Otto had been reported as having been *lightly wounded*, so his death was not caused immediately by war operations; indeed, Otto had been handed to the British as a prisoner of war by his original captors, the French. Thus, *exhaustion* was not even related to combat. In such circumstances, should an inquest have been carried out?

It was the duty of the registrar of deaths, before registering a death, within twelve months of its occurrence to report certain cases (and classes of cases) to the coroner any death which the registrar had reason to believe to have been unnatural or directly or indirectly caused by any sort of accident, violence or neglect, or have been attended by suspicious circumstances or the cause of which appears to be unknown.

Further, if the registrar had reason to believe that it was the duty of some other person to report the death to the coroner, he had to satisfy himself that the death had been duly reported or notified to the coroner.

Then, as now, if a person died in prison it was the duty of the jailer to inform the coroner before the body was buried; for the coroner was required under the Coroners Act 1887 to hold an inquest on the body of every prisoner who died within the prison. *Jervis On Coroners*,[62] the definitive legal text-book of the time, stated:

It is the duty of the coroner in the case of a prisoner dying in prison to hold as full an inquiry into the cause of death as if the death had taken place outside the prison.

Jervis made it very clear that the coroner was well-advised to hold an inquest in any case:

if suspicion can exist, as it well may if a Person die ... in some place that, presents any doubtful or unusual circumstances. The death of a person of unsound mind in... a hospital must be reported by the person in charge of the patient to the coroner before the expiration of the second day after the death.

This was an absolute requirement; it was then up to the coroner to determine whether an inquest was necessary, but Jervis stated that:

it is most desirable that he should cause the usual preliminary enquiries to be made through his officer, and assure himself that nothing is overlooked; it is important that the notification of death to the coroner should not be regarded as a mere formality by any person upon whom the duty is specifically cast.

There were special considerations prevailing in war-time, removing from the jurisdiction of coroners, deaths due to *war operations*, a phrase not strictly defined but held to apply to the armed forces of the enemy or operations of any of His Majesty's forces while in action against the enemy or while acting in the course of their duty upon any warning of

---

[62] This text was in the possession of Pearce Harfield, Solicitors, in 1987, but now is sadly lost

the imminence of any attack by the enemy. Excepting such deaths, arising directly out of combat operations, Jervis said,

it has become useful, and is often realised to be necessary to hold inquests in cases where injuries or disease might have been contracted in, or have been aggravated by war service, whether combatant or non-combatant.

Let us apply these considerations to the facts in this case. Otto's death was definitely not referred to the coroner, and the registrar accepted the certificate of the surgeon who had been attending Otto during his last illness. Given the legal requirements, should Otto really have been treated as a special case, not as a war casualty?

Now, we must turn to the evidence that had been supplied to Otto's family. What sparse information was given to them, conveyed the assertion that he had died following a gastric illness of some sort. The first question which this raises is, *how can this remotely be reconciled with the contents of the death certificate?* According to a War Office memorandum of the 5th July 1915, the Army Council formulated a proposal which Lord Grey's Foreign Office could put to the German authorities via the American Embassy, stating that they were prepared,

on condition of reciprocity, to furnish, as a regular system, in the case of each German prisoner of war and interned civilian dying

In the military hospitals of the British Army in France, or

In hospitals, detention camps in Great Britain, the Colonies, or India,

a Certificate of Death, which would be signed and authenticated by the medical officer who attended the prisoner of war at the time of his death.

Berlin formally agreed the proposal by a Note Verbale dated the 14th December 1915 - exactly one year before Otto's death and, yet, the Scholz family history revealed beyond doubt that they remained unaware of his true causes of death as certified. The British Government apparently failed, in this case, to comply with the agreement which it had, itself, proposed in the first place.

The second question is, *what effect should this conflicting information have had on the decision to conduct an inquest?* It is odd that there was no inquest and the registrar accepted the certificate without further ado of a surgeon, not even a physician. This deepens, of course, when we are reminded of the fact that psychiatry was in its infancy, and an inquest would surely have been desirable, even if only from the point of view of extending the frontiers of medical science? We know, after all, that Netley had been the centre of Army medical research until the Army Medical School was moved to London in 1903. The laboratory was still kept in use, though and with x-rays only just discovered and blood transfusions in their infancy there was still a great deal of work for research and development in an era when medical science simply could not keep up with Man's ingenuity for killing his opponent on as great a scale as possible.

So which was the real cause of death: acute mania or a gastric illness? Which cause of death is more likely to fall within the remit of a Member of the Royal College of Surgeons? If he died of acute mania, it is unlikely that the symptoms manifested rapidly, and he should, therefore, surely, have been repatriated? It seems that detention in solitary confinement was well-known to lead a sound mind to insanity. Was little revealed about Otto because he was, indeed, kept in solitary confinement, for some reason which has not been revealed to us? If he did die in such circumstances, how could a surgeon, not a physician, have been qualified to diagnose such a cause of death? If, however, he died of a stomach complaint, a surgeon may very well have been qualified to diagnose the cause of death, but why was a false statement given on the Death Certificate?

If the family were informed that he died of different causes than those described in the Death Certificate, the obvious question is: *why were they so-informed?* If there were any question of doubt, such could have been resolved by an inquest, but why did the coroner not conduct one in this case? No military or medical records whatever have survived about this important young officer who must have been very interesting both from the military point of view and from the psychiatric point of view, if indeed he was truly insane. Had it not been for the fact that the Registrar of Births Marriages and Deaths in Southampton had an entry of Otto's death in his books, we would never have known that he had died in the asylum at Netley. Should we ask ourselves whether there was something deeper in Otto's fate?

There is one more strand, which arises out of a telephone conversation which the author had in 1987 with a former staff member at Netley. According to him, rumours spread in the Hospital in the 1930's about an Austrian spy who died at Netley and had been buried in *mysterious circumstances* (the witness's words). He associated Otto's story with that of the Austrian spy but, in fairness, Otto had no Austrian connections of which we know, and no corroborative evidence, even of such a rumour, has come to light. It would be safe, therefore, to set this thread aside.

The difficulty that was constantly encountered in this research, was the lack of surviving records; and when records were discovered, they seemed to complicate the case even further. For instance, the Berlin Central Hospital records were located; the entry in the German Casualty List No 837, Issue No 1458 for the 19th May 1917, page 18559, reports Otto's death as a prisoner of war having been hitherto lightly wounded. This raises four important issues:

1. The British did not report Otto's death to the German authorities until May 1917, five months after his death.

2. He was still a prisoner of war at his death, even though his condition as stated in the death certificate must have been so serious as normally to permit such a patient to be sent home as being too seriously disabled to fight further. Hospital beds were needed badly enough for British patients; what was he doing still here?

3. At most, he had been only lightly wounded previously, so what had happened to him?

4. The Casualty List, from the Berlin Central Hospital Records, states that Otto's fate was *bisher nicht bestätigt – not yet confirmed*. In September 1915 Sir Claud Schuster wrote a memorandum about the German casualty lists. It seems that the Germans published certain lists giving the names of prisoners who had been sent back to Germany from France or England as being too seriously disabled to fight further. These detailed lists included references to an entry in an earlier list as to the fate of the man concerned, the place of his former captivity and the place (usually the hospital) in Germany to which he had been sent. If he had not been recorded in a previous casualty list, one could assume that the British had not told the Germans that they had him. If the British had not told anybody that they had Otto, who is to say what had happened to him? The complexity in this argument, though, is that the International Red Cross had information on Otto, so at least they knew about his imprisonment, but when were they told? As Sir Claud Schuster concluded in his memorandum, it was possible that a large number of slightly wounded disappeared without official record. So what were they doing in hospital, in beds much needed for fresh patients from the Front?

One of the major conundrums in this case, involves the issue, raised by the Death Certificate, that Otto was so seriously ill with acute mania, apparently caused or exacerbated by exhaustion, that he should have been repatriated. Just how long would it have taken for him to have become so insane? And what might have induced these symptoms?

It has now been established beyond doubt, that prisoners of war who were unfit for further military service, were regularly exchanged for repatriation, and that this process had been running for over a year before Otto died. The evidence would indicate, further, that Germany gave special consideration to officers whose condition were known to them, when they communicated a request for their repatriation. The War Office considered the request and communicated with the Foreign Office on the 30th June:

Sir,

I am commanded by the Army Council to acknowledge receipt of your communication No S.R.3P/1915 of 26th June, enclosing a copy of a Note Verbale from the German Government concerning four German officers interned in this country, and in reply to acquaint you for the information of Secretary Sir Edward Grey that each of these cases had received careful consideration before the receipt of your letter under reply.

The Council desires to point out that the selection of those prisoners-of-war who are considered unfit for further military service is based entirely on the recommendations, made after careful examination, of the responsible medical officers, and will not be influenced in any way by any representation made by the German Government.

There were four German officers involved, consisting of the following:

1. *Leutnant* Konig, of the Officer Reserve, serving with the 6th Uhlans, who was in Queen Alexandra's Hospital for Officers

in Grosvenor Road, London, having had his left arm amputated above the elbow. He had written to his father, saying that he would be released if a British officer - a Captain Belleville, whose left arm had also been amputated - was also released. The author must ask, How much more tit-for-tat can you get?

2. *Leutnant* Kurt Nickish von Rosenegk, an Engineer with the 5th Pioneer Battalion, who was held at Donington Hall, near Derby.

3. *Leutnant* Ahrens, another Officer in the Reserve, from the 2nd (Kaiser Franz) Grenadier Guards, who had been severely wounded and had written to his wife to say that the doctor in charge of the hospital had said that he was eligible for exchange.

4. *Leutnant* Jakob Schluter, of the 4th Jäger Battalion, was in the Queen Alexandra Hospital with incurable pericarditis.

The sticking point with these four officers was one of procedure, though. The British adopted and abided by a hard and fast rule: the decision as to who should go and who should stay must be that of the examining doctor in the State where the patient was detained, and no effort by the enemy power to repatriate an individual nominated by it would sway that decision. The British doctors decided that *Leutnant* Schluter, mentioned above, and *Fahnrich* (Ensign) Ernst von Schweinichen of the 1st Kurassiers, along with a number of privates, should not be considered incapacitated, and were not exchanged, even though they had been on the list of prisoners to be repatriated.

A furious Note Verbale from Berlin, via the United States Embassy, dated the 16th July 1915, was sent with immediacy following the discovery that a number of the Germans who had been on the list had not been exchanged by the British after all. The Note Verbale referred to a specific response to the British attitude by a note of the German Foreign Ministry of the 31st May, which stated expressly that the final decision in regard to repatriating individuals named in the lists, should be made in neutral Brussels. The note continued:

Leutnant Schluter of the 4th Jäger Battalion and Fahnrich von Schweinichen of the 1st Kurassiers, according to the statements of other disabled prisoners who have returned to Germany, were rejected at the last moment without a thorough investigation being made or reasons given. By the above-mentioned statements, though, Leutnant Schuler's condition is such that a long residence in the English climate has been pronounced as dangerous for him by an English doctor. Fahnrich von Schweinichen must, in the opinion of the English doctors, undergo as soon as possible an operation which cannot be performed in England. The speedy release of these officers, irrespective of the date of the next general exchange, is, therefore, a matter of urgency and is most emphatically requested by the German Government.

The British were entirely unmoved, though. This was when irony stepped in to make an appearance, for, very shortly afterwards, a list of 13 seriously wounded British officers in Germany were put forward to the Foreign Office for repatriation. One of them, Lieutenant J H Brough, of the 8th Battalion Middlesex Regiment, had been reported killed, but in fact had been found by the Germans still alive; he was lying in the Red Cross Hospital at Roulers with both arms amputated, but the last report stated that he was recovering well and would soon be out. Sir Louis Mallet, head of the British Red Cross and Order of St John wrote to the Foreign Secretary on the 21st July:

Sir,

The Prisoners of War Committee of the Red Cross desired me, after their meeting yesterday, to forward to you the enclosed List of Disabled Officers still prisoners in Germany, and to express the strong hope that steps may be taken to procure their exchange as soon as possible. You will observe that some of these officers are totally incapacitated and one of them, Lieutenant Brough, having suffered the amputation of both arms at the shoulders. In regard to this officer, this Department has received many letters from various sources, begging that we should take steps to procure his release and Her Majesty Queen Alexandra has expressed a strong hope that the Society will take up his case, with a view to obtaining his release.

Hoist with their own petard, the Foreign Office had no choice but to decide on the 24th July:

I am afraid that, as we refuse to allow the German Government to suggest German prisoners for exchange, we cannot put forward these names.

On the next day, a senior official in the Foreign Office suggested in a note:

The best plan would be for our Red Cross to represent these cases to the German Red Cross.

Accordingly, the Foreign Office replied to Sir Louis on the 27th July:

The military authorities are very much against either paying any attention to representations about German officers here, or making any representations ourselves. So that if I were to send your letter to the War Office, I am confident that they would advise us to take no action. In these circumstances I suggest that it would be a far better plan if the Red Cross Society were to communicate on the subject of these officers directly with the German Red Cross. But I expect that even they will do nothing, without some promise of reciprocity, which, I fear, will be difficult to obtain.

Two days later, Sir Edward Grey agreed to German proposals that prisoners of war who were unfit for further service to the war effort should be exchanged on a monthly basis, and transported by a neutral Dutch ship, but remained resolute that no special consideration would be given to individuals except by the medical personnel. The most passionate pleas of a mother failed to move him, as Mrs Belleville discovered. Her son, George, was the Captain mentioned so optimistically by *Leutnant* Konig, having been seriously wounded when he was captured. She wrote to Sir Thomas Milvain, an influential man who knew the Foreign Secretary, but, despite even the link with Konig, no ice was cut and Milvain received a reply that:

Under the agreement with the German Government for the exchange of incapacitated prisoners of war, the selection of the persons to be released rests with the Government in whose custody the prisoners are, it is impossible, in the present circumstances, to take any action in the case of particular individuals.

This, of course, rests uncomfortably beside the story of James Sanderson, and the reference to Sir Edward Grey's own relative.

Whether or not it came as a surprise to the Foreign Office, the non-repatriation of Messrs Schluter and von Schweinichen continued to be a thorn in their side, prompting a letter from the War Office of the 28th August, in reply to a letter from the Foreign Office which has now been lost:

As to Schluter and von Schweinichen. We have no wish to detain them in fact should be glad to part with them, if, in the opinion of our medical expert, they were fit subjects for repatriation under the terms of the standard now adopted. We certainly have no wish to bargain with them, nor have we urged particular cases on the German Government and expect similar treatment from them. They were carefully examined by the Medical Board appointed for the purpose after having been selected as subjects for this examination by the medical officer of the 'camp' where they are interned. The decision was made on purely medical grounds and had absolutely nothing to with the non-repatriation of the anticipated number at the time the exchange previous to that of a few days ago was made.

The remarkably defensive tone of this letter begs the question, what, precisely, was said in the missing letter from the Foreign Office?

All patients were considered suitable for exchange if they were:

suffering from severe wounds or illness, whose wounds or complaints are such as to debar them, permanently or for an indeterminate period, from military service in the Army or in the case of officers and NCO's for service in training troops or office work.

Otto's condition clearly satisfied the following criteria for exchange, according to the express terms:

(4)   Damage to the brain with serious results (paralysis of one side or disturbance of important functions of the brain).

(12)   Chronic weakness in consequence of other internal injuries.

(13)   Incurable mental illness.

Given this conclusion, we therefore need to ask the obvious question: *what is the evidence for any proposals for his exchange?* It appears that the British military authorities would have made the decision as to whether he would be involved in an exchange, but how would that have stood in the light of what we know about the limited information that they had given about his condition to the German authorities by that time? The family certainly had not been informed, the Berlin Central Hospital had not been informed, and neither were informed about the certified causes after Otto died. The family was worried and frustrated by the sparse information that the British supplied about Otto; yet, did they not even receive letters from him? It seems that, every month, a prisoner of war could send two letters and a postcard. His whole situation seems to be shrouded in doubt.

Set against such a background, it is apparent, from the evidence of the diplomatic communications between November 1916 and January 1917 of which we have records, that Otto's family had made enquiries about him at the very highest level to ascertain his real situation. Of course, we know that no reply had been received. Yet, behind the scenes, communications between Britain's War Office and their counterparts at the Foreign Office were taking place. In a case beleaguered by lost evidence, the sudden discovery of fresh documents can shed new light on the case – but it has to be interrogated for its probative value. A volunteer group, the Netley Hospital Research Group[63], discovered documents buried deep in the National Archives that Otto had, indeed, been the subject of such a proposal, in exchange with *Lieutenant Gore-Brown who was a prisoner of war in Germany*[64].

In January 1917 the Foreign Office[65] noted that Otto's case was *similar in some respects with that of Lieutenant Gore-Browne*, and that *we had better suggest explicitly that the consideration of this case be made a matter of reciprocity.*

But the Foreign office note added that this was for the War Office to decide.

Undoubtedly one of the most startling pieces of evidence in this whole case, is that the Foreign Office note ended with the question:

If Scholz is really mad, why was he not sent back with the last lot of totally incapacitated?

---

[63] www.netley-military-cemetery.co.uk/

[64] www.netley-military-cemetery.co.uk/german-graves/reh-zeun/

[65] FO383/287

Appended with the date of the 17th January, this final comment clearly indicates that the British Foreign Office had not been informed of Otto's death. And yet the fog of confusion persists, because the Prisoner of War Department in Downing Street was duly approached with the exchange proposals on the 20th January. There is tantalizing corroborative evidence for this. An article in *The Times* on the 3rd July 1915 – eighteen months previously - reported on a visit by a neutral American observer to a prisoner of war camp for Allied officers at Dänholm, Germany. 27 British officers were interned there, including Second Lieutenant Gore-Browne, of the RFA (Royal Field Artillery). The rank is different (although second lieutenants are addressed as Lieutenant) but the surname is spelt differently: Brown is appended with an 'e'. The report commented on the welfare of British prisoners in the camp:

I talked freely with all of them, out of hearing of any German. The British officers live by themselves, occupying two good sized rooms... All seemed well and in good spirits, and all were in communication with their friends at home. All agreed in saying that there was no discrimination against them, and none had any material complaint to make. Letters and parcels are received more promptly than they had been at Mainz. The commandant promised to consider their wishes in regard to the use of a special field for cricket[66].

However, there is a reference to another Gore-Brown (note the spelling of the surname), contained in records in the National Archives: Lieutenant Robert Francis Gore-Brown, Royal Flying Corps, (that is, RFC not RFA) who was interned at Stralsund-Dänholm, Germany. This gives validity to the reference in the Foreign office records[67]. What

---

[66] www.1914-1918.invisionzone.com/forums/index.php?showtopic=116077
[67] FO 383/197

it does reveal, is that, amongst the fog of war, Otto had not been forgotten. But, given the prerequisites for a prisoner exchange to be based upon the permanent incapacity of the individual, it seems strange that no mention is made of Gore-Brown's ill-health in this comfortingly agreeable prison camp. Indeed, a certain Robert Francis Gore-Browne was born in 1893, and lived to a ripe old age, having made a successful career as an author[68], before he died in Hampshire in 1972[69].[70] Perhaps it is pertinent that Gore-Brown(e) came from a family noted in the Peerage, so his family and the Scholz family would have shared similar social status. Is it possible that a discrete exception might have been made in such a case?

Whatever we can make from this evidence, if the seriousness of his condition had not even been reported by the British, there was no realistic likelihood of any special consideration given to his repatriation. But clearly the War Office, which would have taken their information from Netley Hospital, had not passed on vital information about Otto to the Foreign Office, even though diplomatic correspondence had been continuing. In fact, it was not until the 7th February, that the War Office wrote to the Prisoners of War department, stating that Otto had died on the 14th December. No other information was given. The Foreign Office clearly had been anxious to expedite the smooth completion of this exchange, when it suddenly received the news of Otto's death. Their comment was appended in a note on the 7th February, the day the War Office reported the death:

This is most provoking. We wanted to exchange Scholz for Gore-Browne – and now he has died on us.

---

[68] www.gadetection.pbworks.com/w/page/7930678/Gore-Browne,%20Robert
[69] Note his surname had the 'e'
[70] www.imdb.com/name/nm0330718/bio

It then starkly threw the problem to the War Office to explain it all, with a two-word question to the War Office:

What reply?

The trouble with this trail is that it does nothing to explain the fate of Otto Scholz. Let us consider, for a moment, what might have been going on at Netley all the while. Firstly, we must consider the fact that, as the war progressed, it became clear that modern technology had brought warfare to the point where human beings were being maimed and slaughtered by the thousand, soon by the ten thousand and by July 1916 by the million. Surgery had not the first idea of how to compete on these terms. Secondly, we must consider what surgeons believed to be one of the most critical causes of death: simply loss of blood. If the problem could be surmounted, then millions of lives would be saved. What we do know, is that blood transfusions were developed during the First World War and in those days, all that surgery could do was to experiment by trial and error, to try to find a way in the shortest time possible to endeavour to reduce such appalling loss of life.

Mrs Woods recalled with certainty the *scrap shop*, a building within the hospital complex at Netley, standing on its own, where animals were taken *to test them on different things in the pathological room*. What experiments, exactly? Netley was clearly struggling to keep pace with the demands of surgical, medical and psychiatric care in the appalling war for which they had been unprepared, and it would be entirely consistent with good practice to conduct pathological experiments; but how far were the experiments taken?

If Otto had been the subject of experimentation, then it is no wonder that the authorities did not even tell the Foreign Office what was going on, and risk an investigation into a breach of Article 23 of the Geneva Convention:

- In addition to the prohibitions provided by special Conventions, it is especially forbidden

(a) To employ poison or poisoned weapons;
(b) To kill or wound treacherously individuals belonging to the hostile nation or army;

Given the remoteness of such a possibility, Otto's mental condition remains the most troubling aspect of this. It is a fact that much research was taking place into that new casualty of war, the shell-shock victim. We know that the asylum at Netley treated over eight thousand patients during the war, of whom many suffered dreadfully from shell-shock; we also know that close study was made of these most unfortunate victims of war and, as we shall see shortly, evidence of such study survives in the form of silent film footage, doubtless made by pioneering psychiatrists. If we recall the diary accounts taken from captured German officers recording their experiences at the Marne, in September 1914, it is not unreasonable to suggest that Otto was diagnosed as suffering from shell-shock, and conveniently disappeared into the hushed world of the asylum, where the doctors, completely green in matters of psychiatry, could study and carry out their experiments. What is very clear is that the British had not engaged in any dialogue with the German authorities, and so one must ask how they knew of the incurable insanity which Otto may have inherited from his mother, unless Otto told them himself. It might have made sound medical sense to investigate Otto's condition through some tests of trial and error; perhaps, they thought, this was another, hitherto undiscovered, side of war neurosis.

Let us consider this special evidence that it was not only pathological experimentation that was carried out at Netley, for extremely rare footage now under the copyright of the Wellcome Institute was taken at Netley during the First World War[71]. It is extremely moving, but clearly was a film taken by hospital staff officers observing the state of psychiatric patients, and shows how they responded to particular treatment. Retrograde amnesia, hysterical paralysis, hyperadrenalism and fearful standing and walking difficulties typified the symptoms of what was described as *War Neuroses*, the clinical phrase which had been adopted by 1917 to describe shell-shock. Of the patients filmed, none were more tragic than young Private Preston, aged just nineteen, who had contracted amnesia, 'word blindness' and deafness to everything except for the word 'bombs'. He was passive, motionless and quite unresponsive while being spoken to, until he heard the word 'bombs' when he dramatically dived under the bed and then only came out after looking up and all about him, as if he were in the open, looking for signs of shells falling. Another patient had been buried under the earth thrown up by an exploding shell; he had the sort of hysterical gait so typical of shell-shock victims, but it took the authorities five months to send him to Netley for treatment.

One of the most extraordinary features of the film is the claim that patients were cured in a matter of weeks, some of them even in hours. It must be said, of course, that this film witnessed the very birth of military psychiatry, but phrases used, like *persuasion and re-education* have an ominous ring to modern ears, and let us recall the contribution made by Messrs Hurst and Symns, writing in *The Lancet*. The contemporary evidence is conclusive about the prognosis and treatment of shell-shock and it is clear from that evidence that the medical staff would have expected to treat shell-shock victims over very short periods, when, apparently completely cured, they were then sent

---

[71] Held in the custody of the Wellcome Institute; see
https://wellcomecollection.org/works/tpbupwp6

elsewhere to convalesce. The film, surviving today, shows men recuperating at Seaton Hayne Military Hospital, near Newton Abbot in Devon. One wonders whether German shell-shock patients were sent for convalescence; in any event, one can be certain that they would not have been detained long at Netley, for the hospital was always at full capacity, and every bed was desperately needed, so German patients would swiftly have been sent on to prisoner of war camps.

Against this background, we must consider the facts that enable us to draw some reliable conclusions. Clearly, after recovering from the wound suffered when he was taken prisoner, Otto was transferred to the prisoner of war camp at Donington Hall but, subsequently, he appeared to have suffered from some stomach complaint, possibly caused or exacerbated by his light wound when captured, which may have contributed to some general exhaustion and weakness – but that was not the main cause of his death.

The inevitable question then follows, as to how he subsequently died in the asylum, of acute mania, which may originally have been an inherited illness from his mother, but which developed two and a quarter years after his capture. On the strength of medical understanding at the time, the symptoms of 'war neuroses' were eminently curable – but what if the medical team at Netley were investigating whether Otto's insanity was some manifestation of war neurosis that they had to tackle? But of course the question must be put that, if he were so seriously ill, why had he not been repatriated, as was the normal practice for prisoners incapable of further combat? The war was demonstrating medicine's appalling ignorance in the face of the new panorama of casualties and it is both reasonable and likely that research was carried out at Netley in order to alleviate such suffering; it was, after all, one of the leading military hospitals in the world and had ample facilities for experiments. Hearsay evidence of researchers in the 1980's spoke, albeit unreliably, about how eye-witnesses from Netley let slip a reference or two to experimentation and then hastily shut up. It is also a fact that an extremely mysterious but convenient fire in part of the vast hospital building in June 1963 apparently destroyed such records as could disclose such information. The danger, of course, is to weave hypotheses around unreliable evidence, but deep research activity can lead to hypotheses that turn out to be correct.

So, for a moment, let us hypothesise about the fate of Otto Scholz. For all the care which was needed for such a desperately ill man, he was an enemy prisoner of war at a time when they were under increasing strain at Netley with demands for better treatment of the patients coming in daily from the Front. Not many tears would have been shed for him by the British, nor indeed by many of the German rank and file prisoners who saw his class, indeed, his Prussian race, as being the cause of all their troubles both at the Front and at home. His sudden absence would not prompt much protest and, in any event, the asylum was a quiet place, a quarter of a mile from the main complex, and serious cases would have had the benefit of isolation. Some eight thousand patients passed through the asylum during the war, and from surviving statistics, five un-named German patients were confined there in 1915, during the period when Otto may have been there.

With this in mind, let us remember Mrs Woods' recollection:

Poor souls, they had neither ties on nor boot laces. There were many wards in D Block, and padded cells. I think it was always full during war time. They had all their own facilities up there because they did not associate with the other people.

How strange it is that there is not a single surviving scrap of paper in the British Isles that records Otto's medical treatment at Netley. How convenient if he had been safely locked up in the asylum on the grounds that he was violently insane. And how odd that his causes of death should be questioned today by a medico-legal expert who advised (without hearing any prior suggestions on the lines set out above) that 'exhaustion' frequently meant loss of blood.

The weight of evidence inevitably leads us to draw the conclusion that Otto was kept as a prisoner of war, where his mental health deteriorated, possibly compounded by a stomach illness even though that was not a contributing factor to be recorded on his Death Certificate. Anything else would be pure speculation without any evidential foundation that the medical team at Netley had failed their ethical priorities towards him, either through medical negligence or failed experimentation in trial and error which had led to his death. But the very fact of his death, and its causes, should have aroused suspicions of culpable homicide, but those suspicions were concealed from any coroner, and not even the Foreign Office was informed of his death until after his body had been safely buried beyond the danger of any investigation which might reveal the true facts.

In these circumstances, it would certainly not have done to reveal anything more than the most basic information about him, while he was being kept prisoner. He may well have been insane as a result of his inherited condition but, in his captivity, he was treated so badly that he suffered internal injuries, possibly through an operation for his stomach condition, that were consistent with loss of blood - that is, exhaustion, which was covered up in the death certificate to suggest that exhaustion was merely a contributing factor to his cause of death by 'acute mania'.

Netley Hospital in 1900.

Netley Hospital. The Chapel from the same aspect today.

Netley Hospital. The Asylum in 1900.

Netley Hospital. The Asylum, 1987.

Otto Scholz's grave today.

Netley Hospital. The Cemetery today.

NOT A BANG BUT A WHIMPER[72]

On a December Saturday, two days after Otto died, his body was taken along the causeway through the woods to the cemetery. We have no record of any funeral ceremony, although it was customary for enemy officers who died in captivity to be buried with military honours. At least, he was spared the horrors which his family had to endure after 1918, for the war had consequences on his world beyond imagination.

Maybe, it had been borne on a wind that had blown from Russia; but it had a character of its own. In both countries, the economic results of the war had piled hunger and unemployment upon political discontent, but in the mighty country of the Romanovs the suffering of the last three years had been intolerable. In 1914, Russia had put all her meagre supplies of arms into a fast invasion of East Prussia and Galicia. She lost them and a quarter of a million men in September 1914 alone. By 1917 the morale of the Russian Army was despairingly low, while, at home, the appalling administration of a weak and reluctant monarch - who stupidly chose the guidance of his wife over all others around him, and she cared to listen to nobody save for Rasputin - had forfeited the people's confidence in any recovery at all. We need to dwell on this for a moment, because it would have such an enormous consequence on the war, and on the peoples who had fought the war.

By 1917, with supplies of fuel and manpower diverted from industry and agriculture into the seemingly insatiable – and hopelessly incompetent - Russian military machine, the people saw that their

---

[72] T S Eliot, *The Hollow Men*

sacrifices were for nothing, and now even their huge Army was failing. Nicholas was a disastrously poor leader and administrator, and when he left Petrograd in March 1917 to return to Army headquarters at the Front, the administration behind him swiftly disintegrated. Demonstrations spread across the city and, when Cossack troops were called out to cut them down, one Squadron rode off, leaving them undisturbed, while the others refused to press forward, to the applause of the demonstrators. On the next day, the 10th March, the strike in Petrograd became general, and within two days a committee of the Duma formed a Provisional Government with workers electing a *Soviet*.

When Nicholas was first told of these events, he seemed to be incapable of grasping how serious they were. After an agonisingly long delay of three days, he ordered troops loyal to him to go to Petrograd, but they failed to arrive. The most critical scene was now played out: when he tried to return to the Capital himself in his royal train, the way was blocked by troops, so the train had to reverse and divert to Pskov. There, on the deserted station, the Tsar bowed to the unanimous advice of his generals. On the evening of the 15th March 1917, (the Ides of March so fateful for another Caesar) seated alone in his private railway compartment, Nicholas abdicated. Almost 300 years of Romanov rule ended at that moment, but it triggered a series of events that led to the Bolshevik uprising, and a treaty with Germany that took Russia out of the war[73]. This was a God-send to Germany, who would

---

[73] The following year, the Imperial Family was held at the Ipatiev House in Yekaterinburg, Siberia, at the end of their peripatetic imprisonment. On the night of the 16th July, 1918, His Imperial Majesty Nicholas II, the Empress Alexandra, their five children, their physician and three servants were murdered by a firing squad. The local newspaper bragged that Nicholas had been shot without bourgeois formalities but in accordance with our new democratic principles.

now be able to send its armies from the Russian Front to sweep away the Allies in the West, and the 3rd Uhlans rapidly found themselves back on familiar territory on the Western Front, where the trenches had hardly moved since they had left there at the end of September 1914.

Now, at last, the German cavalry could excel in the new rôle that they had carved for themselves, not as horsemen but as the new brand of assault troops in trench warfare that would be refined into Germany's front line fighters of the Second World War. While they shared the two-week routine of manning the trenches alongside the infantry, they also acted as a reserve to reinforce the front line at critical moments, and their effect as crack shock troops gave them a strong psychological advantage, denting the enemy's morale at the time when it was needed most. Dismounted, but still wearing their uhlan tunics, they had abandoned their traditional leather lancer caps for the new *stahlhelm*, as they spearheaded attacks into Allied trenches, armed to the teeth with stick grenades and lethal, often non-standard issue, side-arms.

The success of such units as the Bavarian Chevaulegers, who had remained on the Western Front throughout the war, hastened their evolution from the traditional cavalry function to a new brand of foot-soldier, as they were selected for training in the emerging tactics in which they would become known as stormtroopers, leading the raids on enemy trenches that would leave British veterans with the memory for ever more that trench warfare was mostly a matter of boredom punctuated by moments of panic in struggles for life and death.

But by the time of the Tsar's death, the United States had joined the theatre of war in France, and the German Army had pushed itself to exhaustion. The critical moment struck with the *Kaiserschlacht*, the Spring Offensive of 1918, which so nearly turned the Allied victory into defeat. The storm troopers of the German cavalry now helped to punch a huge advance, throwing back the Allies into headlong retreat. Incredibly, the war graves in the military cemetery at Meaux on the outskirts of Paris have dates in 1914 and again in 1918, mute witnesses to how close Germany came to victory at the beginning and at the end. But then, the exhausted men of the German Army overran a huge British supply depôt. Like stepping into Aladdin's cave, they were overwhelmed by the sight of plenty all around them, and realised that, for the last four years in which they had been fighting, suffering and starving, the Allies had enjoyed all these unbelievable comforts. Such an enemy had surely been fighting with one hand behind its back? Now, with Germany exhausted, all the British had to do, was fight back with the other hand too. The news spread like wildfire and, without any mutiny, or rebellion of any sort, German morale just petered out; the advance ground to a halt, there and then, as half-starved men gorged themselves on food, beer and wine.

The casualty list of the 3rd Uhlans showed just how desperately they tried to advance, but were pushed back in the final months of the war, fighting to the bitter end. Werner Dombois, a *Leutnant der Reserve* like Otto, had fallen at Cirey, near Bouzancourt and Paul Heineman at Ribecourt. *Rittmeister* Albrecht von Roeder had served with the Regiment since they first went into battle in August 1914. He was killed at Pruilly. By his side throughout the war had been *Rittmeister* von Dittmar, who was killed on the 15th August. *Leutnant* Bernhard von der Marwitz followed so many of his family into the Regiment, but was seriously wounded at Bullecourt on the 30th August and died a week later.

By mid-September, the Allies were grinding the German armies into the ground with overwhelming forces, but still they did not break them into headlong retreat. On the 18th September, what was left of the 3rd

Uhlans made a brave stand at Gouzeaucourt. The Regiment lost 70 men dead on the spot. The incredible thing is that they still were not beaten. It was the Kaiser's Government which crumbled away, faced with despair and revolution on the home Front. The Regimental History put it, perhaps, in a soldier's way, describing how, on the 9th November, Revolution broke out in Germany and the country's complete extinction became a possibility; when an armistice - and peace - was agreed. Up until then, the Allies of the Entente - Great Britain and France[74] - were *exhausted and their strategy was at an end, while they could only marvel at the powers of resistance of the German Army*. Now, with total collapse in Germany, the Allies saw that they could demand anything they liked, for Germany was lost.

It was at this time that the German wounded prisoners at Netley felt the loss as tragically as anybody, as 18 Germans died at Netley in these last two months of the war, and the doctors seemed powerless to save them. The thread running through this story, of the sacred duty of the military doctor to save life was now nearing its end. The aristocratic Theophil von Pluto-Prondzinski[75] was a prisoner of war at Netley, like Otto; indeed, both served as Officers in the Reserve, committing themselves to the Teutonic tradition while preparing for a career in civilian life, although Theophil was still undergoing his officer training, and was serving in the ranks as a Corporal. Theophil was in command of an infantry machine gun section, one of those deadly detachments that had made the Somme a scene of martyrdom for the Tommies, but the tide of war had turned dramatically against Germany and, with just weeks left to make a stand, Theophil found himself facing the overwhelming force of the Allied Armies pushing the Germans into retreat. Fighting against a torrent that outclassed the worst that the

---

[74] The Regimental History pointedly put it this way, ignoring the United States
[75] Incorrectly named on his gravestone as von Plotto-Prondzinski

fighting on the Somme could offer, he fell, and was evacuated as a prisoner of war to Netley. He was not there long, though, for he died on the 11th September 1918, aged 24; unlike Otto, he never quite made that last step to an officer, and was buried in the Catholic section of the cemetery. Many more Germans were to follow Theophil in what the doctors at Netley must have considered a shocking and frustrating waste of human life. Max Haase, from the German artillery, died on the same day, while, in the month of October, six more were dead and buried. And still they kept on coming. Georg Schumacher died on All Saints Day, the 1st November, Otto Arnold followed two days later, and Gustav Kanz three days after that. Yet, in less than a week, the fighting would all be over.

To the people of the British Empire, the ceasefire famously came about on the 11th November at 11.00; to the German clocks, it was 12 noon. While the people at home erupted into joy and celebration, the Tommies in the Front Line recalled how an eerie silence descended upon them on the hour. Hardly anybody even spoke; famously, one man remembered he heard just one voice, as a man spoke with hardly more than a sigh,

Well, well.

That day, Max Bolkow and Alwin Zeun died at Netley, and joined a row of German war graves in the cemetery, that epitomises the futility of war. The last prisoner to die at the Hospital was Otto Kerl, on the 17th November 1918. The life and death business at Netley Hospital carried on regardless, as patients were still coming in from the Front, who had been wounded before the Armistice. At Netley they were all too aware that it was an armistice, a cease-fire, not a peace treaty, and it could flare up again[76]. At the end of the month, the nursing service

---

[76] Peace was not cemented until the Treaty of Versailles in 1919.

was confronted with a new challenge:

The Matrons of all the British Military Hospitals… came to my office in the afternoon to discuss various matters in connection with the work of Hospitals. It was impressed upon them that the feeling of restlessness growing up among the Nursing Staff since the signing of the Armistice should be checked; as we are still in a state of war, the services of all are required. In due course orders will be received from the War Office with regard to demobilisation. The Matrons were asked to keep their records well up to date, and not to permit slackness in uniform.

As the guns fell silent at the Front, the 3rd Uhlans stood to in their trench, where they shared the very impression felt by the British in the opposing trenches: a strange feeling – a strange peace, strange despair, strange loss of direction for the foreseeable future. What was different, was the sense of confusion; whoever wrote the words in the Uhlans' Regimental diary had difficulty expressing how strongly they felt this, for to the Germans at the Front they still felt that they were holding out an orderly defence. Eventually, what was left of the 3rd Uhlans loaded up in Brussels in separate sections for the long, long train journey home. They reached Fürstenwalde on the 20th November. But it had become a different place; the whole of Germany had become a different place. The country was on its knees, and a revolution was on its way to Berlin. The fate of Russia, so recently hoped for and welcomed by the Kaiser's High Command, now turned and cast its shadow upon Germany.

Economically, the situation did not seem so bad. Real wages in Germany were 77 per cent of what they had been in 1914; even in the United Kingdom, they were not far behind at 85 per cent. The difference lay in the respective blockades, for Germany was starving, with a food shortage that increased food prices in an inflationary spiral, so that, what food there was, was unobtainable by the mass of unskilled workers and families at home. It had not escaped their notice, though, that the food situation had actually enriched farmers, under the old laws of supply and demand. Moreover, as the war dragged on, the captains of heavy industry were enjoying prosperity as they could name their own prices to a government which had to have their products at all costs, for the war effort.

The Revolution broke out as the result of despair and hardship; but when it came to hardship, they had not seen anything yet. The skilled industrial workers had been making good wages while the war was on, but now, with hostilities at an end, and no marketplace left for their products, where would they be? Then the soldiers came home - or, rather, the survivors, for just 59 per cent of those who went to war, came back in one piece. 2.7 million Germans had been killed, another 4 million had been maimed and unable to support themselves or their families. Of those who could work, where were the jobs? At least, families would have their savings to tide them over. Or would they? The war had mostly been financed by issuing war bonds which, the government promised, would be paid back to the people with handsome interest, by the vanquished Allies. It became a patriotic duty to commit your savings to war bonds. Now the government had no money with which to repay those loans and, with war reparations to pay, there was no hope on the horizon that it could find the money. Inflation had already increased by 250 per cent and soon it would gallop away uncontrollably. Nobody had any savings any more.

Economic hardship hit the middle classes hardest of all, for they had committed the most to war bonds, and they now looked forward to the fewest jobs. They looked at the privileged classes who had profited out of the ever-growing agricultural prices; they looked at the big businessmen who had made fortunes in industry; they looked at the blue-collar workers who forced their unions to strike for more pay - and the industrialists promptly had agreed to their demands. It was the liberal middle classes who quickly learned what the Russian lesson could do for them, and gave birth to the Social Democrats of the November Revolution. But this new child quickly turned out to be a Sorcerer's Apprentice. Workers' and Soldiers' Councils sprang up spontaneously as vehicles of self-government in a political whirlwind that might otherwise be described as chaos. The Left clashed with the Far-Left, leaving the old dynasties such as the Scholz family to make it through the cross-fire as best they could. In January 1919, things became more frightening still when violent fighting by the Far-Left broke out in Berlin and, within days, uprisings and attempted revolutions broke out like an epidemic in cities across Germany.

This was not a good time for Otto's family. Berlin was a city of ghosts now, where anarchy reigned. But Silesia, their old family home, offered no future, either, only despair. Opportunist insurrections by Poles paid off and they brought the upper lands into the new Polish Republic. When the war-weary soldiers of Silesia returned to the Scholz family homeland, they were barely able to fight off the uprisings, but held on to their old Prussian provinces, before the League of Nations organised a plebiscite to decide the issue in 1921, which resulted in 60 per cent of votes being cast for Germany and 40 per cent for Poland. This just opened a gaping wound further though and, later in 1921, there was yet another uprising in Silesia and, this time, the easternmost portion of Upper Silesia, with a majority ethnic Polish population, was awarded to Poland. The old Prussian Province of Silesia within Germany was then divided into the provinces of Lower Silesia and Upper Silesia, while Austrian Silesia, the small portion of Silesia retained by Austria after the Silesian Wars, was mostly absorbed into the new Republic of Czechoslovakia, with the rump going to Poland.

The old Scholz homeland in Silesia was barely the place they remembered any more, and so, it seems, the family braced itself for the lesser of two evils and remained in the broken Imperial Capital for a while. At least, there, they still had a living. Otto's father had risen to Senate President of the Upper Administrative Court, but also with a much more mysterious appointment to the *Geheimer Oberregierungsrat*, the Cabinet to the Government. Research so far has shed little light on this but, in 1919, he did write a monograph on police legal risk[77]. At the time of writing a copy has not been discovered.

Otto's mother died in Berlin in November 1921. His father held on to his values, and changed the family name to Scholz-Forni on the 14th March 1923, before he died, aged 78, on the 24th July 1925, at Bad Braunlage, a health resort in Lower Saxony. Otto's younger sister, Amelie, married a banker, Walter von Karger, in Berlin, on the 28th March 1940. But no member of the Scholz family has been traced in Berlin today.

If you walk down Ranke Straße today, you will find yourself in a broad, tree-lined boulevard, running south from the opulent Kurfustendamm from the square where the famous ruins of the Kaiser Wilhelm Memorial Church now stand. In 1987 enquiries were made with the occupiers of 13 Ranke Straße, the last address which the Red Cross had for Otto's father, a firm of lawyers who had been there since 1957. They said that, at the outbreak of war in 1939, there was no Scholz living there and during the war the building was badly bombed, with only one wing survived. Today, it is a modern office block housing a car park management company. In fact, the only idea which we might have of the opulence of Otto's house can be suggested by one, very

---

[77] Scholz-Forni, O, 1919, Die Polizeirechtliche Gefahr, in Verwaltungsarchiv (VA), Bd. 27, 1919, S. 1-84

grand, private house on the opposite side of the boulevard, which survived the bombing of the Second World War.

It is amazingly bad luck that every document that could help us with tracing the family, seems to have been lost or destroyed. In Germany, bombing raids in 1944 destroyed military records that might have told us so much and, despite the superb efforts of the British Consul-General in West Berlin and the British Consul in East Berlin in the early years of research into this story, no trace of the family could be found. The West Berlin Police tried hard to trace his relatives, without success; while, despite coverage in the leading newspaper *Berliner Morgenpost* in 1989, not a single relative, friend or anybody else has come forward.

Otto was not forgotten by his brother, Robert, who erected a fine tombstone on Otto's grave at Netley in 1938; it is there today. We do know that Robert settled with his wife, Renata, in her home town of Hamburg, and became a businessman, living at No 10 Blumen Straße. In the same year that Robert arranged for Otto's private tombstone, his beautiful wife died; but they had four fine children, three girls and a boy. Robert Scholz-Forni became an Honorary Senator of the City of Hamburg, where he died in 1963, but traces of the family story since then have been hard to find and conflicting. Their son, whom they named Otto, was born in 1925; recently discovered records reveal that he died in 2011 aged 85[78]; sadly, the records do not reveal whether he had any surviving children.

Robert had a fine art collection, which found itself in some peril at the end of the Second World War, under the threat of Soviet Russian invaders who undoubtedly would have pillaged it. Accordingly, he dispersed the collection between his house and the houses of Herr

---

[78] https://www.myheritage.com/names/otto_scholz-forni

Berghotz, Herr Heinrich and Herr von Fackh[79]. It was duly saved for the family, and boasted among its treasures *The Royal Hunt of Dido and Aeneas*, a famous painting by the Italian artist Francesco Solimena which was acquired by the Museum of Fine Arts in Houston, Texas[80]. In 1954, Robert sold a portrait of Donna Alba Regina del Ferro by Giacomo Ceruti to the Metropolitan Museum in New York[81]; perhaps they were family heir-looms, a legacy of the Forni family, all that was left of the beautiful collection of art which had been such a joy to the family over the generations.

Netley Military Hospital hardly outlived those whom Otto had known. Its record in the First World War had been a remarkable achievement; it was, indeed, the Hospital's finest hour. But, once that hour had passed, in 1918, Netley's fate passed into shadow. At first, it seemed that the timeless routine of the pre-war years would be restored but, in fact, the sudden drop in traumatised patients presented an anti-climax in much the same way as survivors at the Front felt a dreadful anti-climax following the 11th November. There were no more hospital trains full of fresh casualties from the Front; but patients were still dying. As the war drew to a close, the German wounded prisoners of war at Netley seemed to give up; an almost-unbroken line of nine German tombstones in the cemetery marks the graves of those who just seemed to give up the ghost.

In Haig's Somme dispatch in December 1916, he praised the work of the medical services in their desperate efforts to meet the demands of the battle:

---

[79] T 209/21/1

[80] https://www.christies.com/lotfinder/Lot/francesco-solimena-canale-di-serino-1657-1747-barra-4109520-details.aspx

[81] https://www.christies.com/lotfinder/Lot/giacomo-ceruti-milan-1698-1767-portrait-of-5221720-details.aspx

The losses entailed by the constant fighting threw a specially heavy strain on the Medical Services. This has been met with the greatest zeal and efficiency. The gallantry and devotion with which officers and men of the Regimental medical service and Field Ambulances have discharged their duties is shown by the large number of the R.A.M.C. and Medical Corps of the Dominions who have fallen in the Field. The work of the Medical Services behind the front has been no less arduous. The untiring professional zeal and marked ability of the surgical specialists and consulting surgeons, combined with the skill and devotion of the medical and nursing staffs, both at the Casualty Clearing Stations in the Field and the Stationary and General Hospitals at the Base, have been beyond praise[82].

The end of Netley Hospital was no swift thing, but never again did it play such a leading part in history, and in a generation the front line of army nursing left it far behind. The main hospital had been closed some five years when, at 02.16 on the 25th June 1963, Sergeant Dennis Keating noticed a fire in a disused part of the main block at Netley and immediately called Hamble Fire Station. Within minutes the first fire engine was on the scene, to find some 150 feet by 120 feet of the front wing well alight on the second and third floors. Within a minute of the first call to Hamble, three more fire engines were ordered from Southampton and were on their way within the next minute. 12 jets of water played on the fire and a 100-foot turntable was in attendance, with a fireboat waiting offshore pumping extra water to the fire. 75 firemen prevented the blaze from engulfing the main part of the building and only the front wing was affected. After the fire, a Hampshire Fire Service spokesman told the local newspaper, the *Echo*: *So far there is nothing to indicate the cause of the fire.*

Privately, though, it was confided to somebody that the fire had been

---

[82] See www.1914-1918.net/haigs_somme_dispatch.htm

started with professional efficiency. The full report of the fire brigade would throw much light on the cause of the fire and the extent of the damage; but exhaustive enquiries failed to discover a copy.

Maybe we should put some pieces together, here. We know that in January 1956, the commander in chief of the Army in the southern area, General Sir George Erskine, suggested that the main building of the hospital was *a shocker*, since it was out of date and required £50,000 to keep it watertight and painted. The local press reported that the general felt,

It is uneconomic to maintain such a building and thinks that it would be better if it were pulled down even to make hard core for roads.

Strangely enough, the building was not destroyed completely by the fire, in fact only the central part had been destroyed, and much of the building had been unharmed, for the fire brigade had done its job very well. Yet, the authorities agreed, it should be razed to the ground, despite local protests, and despite the fact that, unbelievably, the roof had only just been renewed. Only the Chapel was to remain, the focal point of the new country park.

The only thing to remain above ground, any way... For there was once a story, told by Park staff thirty years ago, that, long after the building had been demolished, a drain engineer was called to sort out some flooding. In the course of his inspection, he discovered an entrance to an underground tunnel, that led into some rooms, operating theatres maybe, that still remained there. It seemed to be something which the powers that be had forgotten. The really interesting bit, is that it was unknowingly corroborated by a former employee of the Hospital, Mr Pool, who had not been asked about the story when he recalled that underneath the hospital was a long corridor, a tunnel with all the services and everything, where the wild cats lived. Maybe, it was here, where experiments had been carried out during the First World War. Who knows?

And the asylum? At about the same time, the old asylum building was renovated, redeveloped and taken over by Hampshire Constabulary, to become a police training college. Modern architecture has served to enhance the central core of its beauty, and it stands in the grounds, still surrounded by the old asylum's high, brick perimeter wall, where Otto Scholz drew his last breath, that fateful day, the 14th December, 1916.

EPILOGUE

An Epilogue is designed to bring closure to a book. Before we do that, let us take one step more, to understand the aftermath, with a glimpse of Britain in the years after the War's end. By the 1930s, the War was receding in people's memory: the world was moving on, and society had to look to the next sunrise. This was most graphically portrayed in the art deco movement, the clean, minimalist architecture and the sunrise motif that appeared everywhere – somehow reflecting the new mood, in which society shunned the Old Order and, instead, embraced an entirely new ambition for itself, that would defy any attempt by Governments and Powers to force them into brutalisation again. There would be no more war.

No more clearly was this witnessed than in the Oxford Union undergraduate debate in 1933 which characterised the feeling of the post-War years, and carried a motion that *This House would not in any circumstances fight for King and Country*. It could hardly have come as a surprise that it shocked the Establishment to the core, which sought to restore the comfortable pre-War status quo in society that relied on obedience to Class and its associated boundaries to power. Yet, the undergraduates were hardly representative of the starving workers rising up in Moscow or the German soldiers returning home to a shattered State of anarchy. These students were largely from wealthy upper- or middle-class families; they were highly literate and well-read; and they were more prepared than most people to engage with abstract issues of principle. Churchill was outraged by the motion but, as Churchill College (Cambridge) observes,

Oxford and Cambridge undergraduates were an influential group, far

more so than they are today. They were regarded – rightly – as the rising stars of politics and both the press and politicians took an interest in what the students were saying, especially in their debating societies. [83]

The Oxford Union debate demonstrates hope that a brutalised society can still abound in hope, that never more would there be another war to bring the civilised world to its knees.

Just two weeks before, Hindenburg had offered Hitler the chancellorship of Germany.

Now, with all the evidence before us, we need to see how far we have come in this book, and make our final judgment on the fate of Otto Scholz. It means reaching a conclusion in our mind about how Netley Hospital responded to the War, and how the demands of trying to save life put stresses on its sacred duty to serve human life and health. The golden thread running through this story has been all about how friend and foe faced each other; how they were brought there from the Front by the thousands, some in khaki, some in grey, still bloody and caked in mud; and how the Hospital coped with that, facing a changing psychology of war, amidst the normative ethics of a society that had been brutalised by it.

In his academic paper *The Homicide Ladder*[84], Victor Tadros observed a vital feature about human attitude towards loss, when he said that *When death is caused it is a natural reaction to look around for someone to blame.* In the painful years following the Armistice in 1918, when the loss and the pain was still so raw, writers and analysts, seeking to rationalise the final outcome, put all their energy into questioning just

---

[83] See www.chu.cam.ac.uk/archives/education/churchill-era/exercises/appeasement/appeasement-public-opinion/

[84] Tadros, V, Modern Law Review (2006) 69(4) MLR 601-618, at 601

who was responsible for the outbreak of the war and the conduct of the protagonists from their High Commands across Europe.

A century later, the generation of those who suffered that loss and pain has passed away. The focus of writers has turned, instead, to ploughing over well-furrowed fields of historical material, in order to challenge the accepted view, and ask one of two questions: *Is that right?* Or, *That can't be right?* The key is to reassess the culture of 1914-18, or as much of it as they can piece together from what has been preserved by historians and museum archives. The aim of this book, has been to uncover the emotions forged by the consciousness of that generation that has now been laid to rest, analysing the popular mentalities that drove the conflicting national feelings that took European societies to war[85]. It was, after all, their social ethics that created the society of 1914. What was left of those ethics to drive the peace of 1918? Modern historians, freed from the shackles of a society still looking for someone to blame for their loss, can open a new frontier, hardly touched, by challenging how perception and consciousness shaped reality and common experience in the First World War. The result which challenges us today is, no doubt, unexpected, and startling. It reveals that the deaths and horrifying injuries, all the experiences of war inflicted on an industrial scale by modern technology, triggered by remote fingers on howitzers and machine guns, had the effect of brutalising a society that had been childishly innocent just four years previously.

What of the military doctors and nurses who had to fight on the other side of this technology? They had to struggle to close their minds to

---

[85] Le Tallec, Y, Historiography of World War One. On-line source of the British Library, see www.bl.uk/world-war-one/articles/historiography-of-world-war-one#authorBlock1

the tidal wave of horror before them and stem the flow of blood from friend and foe. Its people all passed long ago, but its silent witnesses remain to tell their story, all the same, and you will find them, neatly spaced in regulation rows, in the Hospital's cemetery. Friend and foe lay silently beside each other and, without the consciousness of their generation's pain and suffering, you wonder how that generation must have felt.

And that's the start of it, for we have had to wrestle with the question of how the medical teams of doctors, surgeons and nurses could remain above the fray. When confronted with the fearful waves of wounded, flooding in from the Western Front, would you or I have turned our faces from the medical ethics of a peacetime world? That had been a world which could not have dreamed the nightmare of a frantic struggle, to staunch a stream that never seemed to end, of patients who depended on your skill to save their lives without the technology for a blood transfusion; a world which had never thought through the effect which a million roars of gunfire could have upon a human mind which knew of no escape.

There would never be just cause to harm a person out of prejudice for friend or foe, there would never be cause to inflict harm on the few in the endeavour that the many shall live. There would never be cause to turn a blind eye to such duty for the cause of one's own society, or country. As an embodiment of these tenets, the Hippocratic Duty has shone the way for doctors since ancient times who must remain as inviolable in war as in peace:

I swear.... I will carry out, according to my ability and judgment, this oath and this indenture.

I will use treatment to help the sick according to my ability and judgment, but never with a view to injury and wrong-doing. Neither will I administer a poison to anybody when asked to do so, nor will I suggest such a course. Similarly I will not give to a woman a pessary to cause abortion. But I will keep pure and holy both my life and my art. I will not use the knife, not even, verily, on sufferers from stone, but I will give place to such as are craftsmen therein.

Into whatsoever houses I enter, I will enter to help the sick, and I will abstain from all intentional wrong-doing and harm, especially from abusing the bodies of man or woman, bond or free.

Did they meet their sacred duty at Netley? That is the question that still hangs over the grave of Otto Scholz.

BIBLIOGRAPHY

Anon, Rangliste der Königlich Preussischen Armee für 1913, Ernst Siegfried Mittler und Sohn, Berlin

Anon, British Vessels Lost at Sea 1914-1918, HMSO, first published 1919

Bloem, W, 2011 (reprint), The Advance from Mons 1914: The Experiences of a German Infantry Officer, Helin & Company

Bronner, F (updated by A Lid), 2013, The Royal Bavarian 2nd Chevauleger Light Cavalry

Brown, M and S Seaton, 1994, Christmas Truce, Pan, London

Bucher, G, 2006 (reprint), In the Line, Naval & Military Press

Burrows, W, 1972, Richthofen, Mayflower, London

Cohen, S, 2014, Medical Services in the First World War, Bloomsbury, London

Clausewitz, C, 1832, On War, unfinished but published posth by his widow

Conolly, N, 1890, Acute Confusional Insanity, Read before the Section of Medicine in the Royal Academy of Medicine in Ireland, on Friday, May 16, 1890, collection King's College London

Cron, H, 2006, Imperial German Army 1914-1918, Helion & Co, Solihull

Crutchley, C, 1975, Machine Gunner 1914-1918, Purnell, London

Daniels, S, 1993, Enemies At Peace, Hampshire

Derby, I, Manic-depressive "exhaustion" deaths: An analysis of "exhaustion" case histories. Psychiatric Quarterly, 1933;7:436–49

Elting, J, 1997, Sword Around A Throne, Perseus Books

Gerster, M, 1920, Das Württembergische Reserve-Infanterie-Regiment, Nr. 119 im Weltkrieg, 1914-1918, C. Belsersche

Verlagsbuchhandlung, Stuttgart

Gilbert, M, 2006, The Somme: Heroism and Horror in the First World War, Henry Holt, New York

Holder, J, 1981, Royal Victoria Country Park, Hampshire County Council, Winchester

Horton, C (D le Vack ed), 2013, Stretcher Bearer, Lion Hudson, Oxford

Hurst & Symns, 1918, Hysterical Symptoms in Soldiers, The Lancet, London

Jones, Prof E and Prof S Wessely, War Syndromes: The Impact of Culture on Medically Unexplained Symptoms, Med Hist 2005 Jan 1; 49(1): 55–78

Marrion, R, 1974, Lancers and Dragoons: Uniforms of the Imperial German Army, Almark

Masters, J, 1956, Bugles and a Tiger, Michael Joseph, London

Masur, G, 1974, Imperial Berlin, Taylor & Francis, Abingdon

Melville, M, 1981, The Story of the Lovat Scouts, St Andrew Press, Edinburgh

Middlebrook, M, 1971 (2016), The First Day on the Somme, Penguin Books, London

Miller-Keane Encyclopedia and Dictionary of Medicine, Nursing, and Allied Health

Poseck, M von, 1923, The German cavalry in 1914 in Belgium and France, republished 2007 Naval and Military Press, Uckfield, E Sussex

Prior, R and T Wilson, 1992, Command on the Western Front: The Military Career of Sir Henry Rawlinson 1914–1918, Blackwell, London

Rangliste de Koniglich Preussischen Armee fur 1913, Ernst Siegfried Mittler und Sohn, Berlin

Scholz-Forni, O, 1919, Die Polizeierechtliche Gefahr in Verwaltungsarchiv (VA), Bd.27, 1919, S.1-84

Scholz-Forni, R, 1941, Die Scholz-Forni und ihre Anverwandten, Hamburg

Scotland, T and S Heys, 2014, Understanding The Somme 1916, Helion & Co, Solihull

Shaw, M, How did soldiers cope with war? On-line source of the British Library

Smith, Dr T, 1915, The Soul of Germany: A Twenty Year Study of the people from Within, 1902-14, Grosset & Dunlop, New York

Tadros, V, Modern Law Review (2006) 69(4) MLR 601-618, at 601

Tuchman, B, 1962, The Guns of August, reprinted 2009 Random House

Zipfel, E, 1931, Geschitchte des Ulanengeiments 'Kaiser Alexander II von Russland' (1 Brandenburgischen) nr 3, Zeulenroda, Thuringen

UK ARCHIVE RECORDS

National Archives documents:
Air Force Administration: ADM/273/8/147
Prisoners of war: FO 383/287; 383/420
Medical records: MH106
Treasury Records: T 209/21/1
Unit war diaries: WO 95/1-3154; 3911-4193; 1112/1; 1495; 5500
Gallantry awards: WO 98
Intelligence reports and summaries: WO 157
Reports of Prisoners of war: WO 161
Specimen lists of British prisoners of war in the UK WO 900/45

Hampshire County Records Office documents:
Hospital records: 92M91/2; 92M91/5

The Wellcome Institute, London
For guidance, see:
www.wellcomelibrary.org/collections/about-the-collections/archives-
and-manuscripts/

ON-LINE SOURCES

https://wellcomecollection.org/works/tpbupwp6www.bl.uk/world-war-one/articles/historiography-of-world-war-one#authorBlock1

www.economist.com/news/21663911-what-we-wrote-her-passing-1901-death-queen-victoria

www.lib.byu.edu/index.php/Agadir_Crisis:_Lloyd_George's_Mansion_House_Speech

www.nam.ac.uk/explore/british-army-horses-during-first-world-war

www.2chevauleger.org/Resources/Bavchevbook2013.pdf

www.wellcomelibrary.org/item/b18618157

www.ezitis.myzen.co.uk/southafrican.html

www.bac-lac.gc.ca/eng/discover/military-heritage/first-world-war/personnel-records/Pages/item.aspx?IdNumber=184042

www.bjp.rcpsych.org/content/90/380/761

www.launcestonthen.co.uk/launcestonsfallenfromworldwarone.html

www.bl.uk/world-war-one/articles/how-did-soldiers-cope-with-war

www.netley-military-cemetery.co.uk/

www.1914-1918.invisionzone.com/forums

www.gadetection.pbworks.com/w/page/7930678/Gore-Browne

www.naval-history.net/WW1NavyBritishBVLSMN1501.htm

www.imdb.com/name/nm0330718/bio

www.1914-1918.net/haigs_somme_dispatch.htm

www.chu.cam.ac.uk/archives/education/churchill-era/exercises/appeasement/appeasement-public-opinion/

www.myheritage.com/names/otto_scholz-forni

ACKNOWLEDGMENTS

Grateful thanks are given to the following for their generous assistance and for the primary source material in their care:

Mr Ashley Ailes, Barrister

Botschaft der Bundesrepublik Deutschland, Copenhagen and London

British Consulate-General, Berlin

British Embassy, East Berlin (as it then was)

Bundesarchiv Militaerarchiv

Comité International de la Croix Rouge

Commonwealth War Graves Commission

Deutsche Dienstelle (WASt)

Hampshire County Council

Hampshire Constabulary, both Police Headquarters Winchester and the staff at Netley

Mr William Hewitson, Barrister

Krankenbuchlager, Berlin

Militaergeschichtliches Forschungsamt

National Archives of Canada

Netley Hospital Research Group

Public Records Office (Now the National Archive)

Vic Puik

Rechtsanwaltskammer, Berlin

Senator fur Inneres, Berlin

Southampton City Coroner

Southampton City Reference Library

Southampton Registrar of Births Marriages and Deaths

Southampton and South West Hampshire Health Authority

Southern Newspapers plc (The Echo)

Springer Foreign News Service, London

Standesamt 1 to 13 inclusive, Berlin

Volksbund Deutsche Kriegsgrabefursorge

The Wellcome Institute:

Important archive material on the treatment of shell-shock victims at
   Netley

Wolfgang Franzelius Ingrid-Leonore Thur-v Schultz, Berlin

ABOUT THE AUTHOR

Dr Simon Daniels qualified as a Solicitor in 1985, practising in litigation, before he brought his professional background to Solent University, where he managed the law and business parts of the Merchant Vessel Operations programme at Warsash Maritime Academy. In 2012, he was awarded a PhD for his thesis: *The Criminalisation of the Ship's Master: A new approach for the new millennium.*

Simon has close associations with the Royal Victoria Country Park, the site of the former hospital where this drama took place. In 2016, he gave a presentation commemorating the part which the Hospital played in caring for the wounded from the Somme campaign, and in 2018 delivered a series of presentations in the Chapel commemorating the centenary of the Armistice.

Printed in Great Britain
by Amazon

44597605R00151